SEND IN THE CLONES

Studies in Popular Music

Series Editors: Alyn Shipton, journalist, broadcaster and former lecturer in music at Oxford Brookes University, and Christopher Partridge, Professor of Religious Studies, Department of Politics, Philosophy and Religion at Lancaster University

From jazz to reggae, bhangra to heavy metal, electronica to qawwali, and from production to consumption, Studies in Popular Music is a multi-disciplinary series which aims to contribute to a comprehensive understanding of popular music. It will provide analyses of theoretical perspectives, a broad range of case studies, and discussion of key issues.

Published

Open Up the Doors: Music in the Modern Church
Mark Evans

Technomad: Global Raving Countercultures
Graham St. John

Dub in Babylon: Understanding the Evolution and Significance of Dub Reggae in Jamaica and Britain from King Tubby to Post-Punk
Christopher Partridge

The Lost Women of Rock Music: Female Musicians of the Punk Era
Helen Reddington

Forthcoming

Global Tribe: Technology, Spirituality and Psytrance
Graham St. John

Heavy Metal: Controversies and Countercultures
Edited by Titus Hjelm, Keith Kahn-Harris and Mark LeVine

SEND IN THE CLONES

A CULTURAL STUDY OF THE TRIBUTE BAND

GEORGINA GREGORY

Published by Equinox Publishing Ltd.

UK: Kelham House, 3 Lancaster Street, Sheffield, S3 8AF
USA: ISD, 70 Enterprise Drive, Bristol, CT 06010

www.equinoxpub.com

First published 2012 by Equinox Publishing Ltd.

British Library Cataloguing-in-Publication Data
A catalogue record for this book is available from the British Library.

Library of Congress Cataloging-in-Publication Data
Gregory, Georgina.
Send in the clones : a cultural study of the tribute band / Georgina Gregory.
p. cm. -- (Studies in popular music)
Includes bibliographical references and index.
ISBN 978-1-84553-263-5 (hb) -- ISBN 978-1-84553-245-1 (pb)
1. Tribute bands (Musical groups) 2. Popular music--History and criticism. I. Title.
ML3470.G74 2011
781.64--dc22
2011004422

ISBN 978-1-84553-263-5 (hardback)
978-1-84553-245-1 (paperback)

Typeset by CA Typesetting Ltd, www.sheffieldtypesetting.com
Printed and bound in the UK by MPG Books Group

Contents

List of Figures

Acknowledgements

Thanks to all the musicians who were kind enough to provide me with their personal insights and information about their work. Special thanks must go to Steve Elson, Wayne Ellis, Jose Maldonado, Danielz, Wanda Ortiz, Adrian Gregory, Steph Paynes, Dave (Sex Pistols Experience) and Paul Higginson. Kevin Ryan of Charnwood Arts very kindly allowed me to use images and I would like to thank Christopher Popa and Ed Wincentsen for being prepared to share their expert knowledge with me. Colleagues at University of Central Lancashire and elsewhere have all been tolerant of my obsession and deserve a mention: John Walton, Dave Russell, Anandi Ramamurthy, Susan Sydney-Smith, Fazila Bhimji and in particular – Ewa Mazierska – all of you have helped me in different ways. Thanks go to Pat Walsh for illuminating observations. Friends too, have been really supportive – Kath, Hazel, Tony, Sue, Bertie, Ines – accompanying me on nights out or being prepared to listen to endless tales about men in leather trousers! I am grateful to Alyn Shipton for guidance and patience throughout the project and my children must be also given credit for their patience and support. Finally, I would like to dedicate this book to my mother and my late father for their love and encouragement over the years.

1 Introduction

A glance at any local newspaper will reveal a variety of tribute bands playing in venues ranging from the small pub or local live music club, to concerts in larger regional theatres and stadiums. In 2005 it was estimated that there were more than 10,000 tribute bands in England alone and these numbers have most likely swelled as the bands continue to multiply in a gradually maturing scene.[1] The majority of them will only ever attain a modest level of success within what has become an increasingly competitive industry: with the advent of cheaper equipment and the internet, it is pretty easy to try out launching a mimetic enterprise. However a small minority do go on to achieve international stardom. For instance, Bjorn Again, referred to in certain quarters as the "Manchester United" of the parody acts, can command concert fees of up to £150,000 a night while The Bootleg Beatles, formed from the cast of the musical *Beatlemania*, are now in their twenty-fifth year.[2] Moreover, although dubbed the "Faux Four," with the benefit of new technology, they have managed to surpass their fab counterparts with live performances of music once restricted to a studio setting solely.[3]

Tributes may enjoy lengthy careers performing the repertoire of the icons of rock and pop but, regardless of their popularity or the relative longevity of their respective careers, these signifiers of success have failed to guarantee them a place within the various histories of popular music. They are not alone in being excluded. Most studies of popular music defer to the hegemony of the multi-nationals by exaggerating the importance of signed artists and their tangible products – the record or CD, but in doing so, they fail to identify, let alone award merit, to the amateur and semi-professional musicians whose contribution to the everyday enjoyment of music is significant.

If we look at this area of entertainment – apart from work carried out by Homan (2006), scholarly interest is limited and, as already noted, the phenomenon is generally ignored in music histories as well, but then, as Thornton (1990) argues, the magnitude attached to popular music is designated according to a particularly limited set of criteria. Biographical interest, critical reception, media coverage and those all-important record sales figures are the main yardsticks and, as tribute acts fail to fit within the benchmarking system, they are effectively invisible. In the "totalizing" or linear histories of popular music, artists, styles and genres are recorded in a quasi-Old Testament manner. The univocal approach is a litany which drowns out any competing voices, especially those of female or non-white artists, and needless to say these works contain no information about tribute and cover bands or the artists who perform in them. In a revisionist plea, female band The Pipettes, make a spirited call for reform:

> Let us write the histories of pop music (the plural has a certain importance). A history at once oral/aural but not linear or progressive. A history that snakes and twists and turns back on itself, a history of ruptures and wrong-turnings. But let us not start with The Beatles ... There is a traditional historiography of popular music which in some way or another always seems to come back to The Beatles; and Lonnie Donegan who begat The Beatles, and Elvis who begat Lonnie Donegan, John Lee Hooker who begat Elvis and Robert Johnson who begat John Lee Hooker etc. etc. (www.thepipettes.co.uk/).

One of the main problems with the creationist narrative and the obscurity of those on the margins is that, "the cultural experiences of large parts of the population who are not in tune with the tastes of music critics or not already represented in the music press will be lost" (Thornton 1990: 87). Disregarding the omnipresence of repetition as an accepted practice within an industry which invented the cover version, and where definitive versions are oft-disputed, the primacy of the author and their identity are carefully protected for the system deliberately plays down the significance of unauthored performance.

In failing to acknowledge the importance of the tribute in a cultural climate hell-bent on the commodification of identity, popular music histories are swimming against a tidal wave of popular entertainment based upon the re-enactment of celebrity characters and rags to riches narratives. Consider for example, the growth of look alike agencies which will hire out a "David Beckham" or a "Michael Jackson" for the evening and television programmes like *Stars in Their Eyes*, where amateurs perform the work and identity of the icons of pop and rock. Then there are the formulaic TV talent shows such as *X Factor* and *American Idol*, whose appeal is dependent on the interest generated in the entertainment value of talented amateurs. We love nothing better than stories of successful underdogs whose talent enables them to win against all odds. How great, for example, are the chances of being picked out of obscurity from paying homage to your favourite band and playing with them in real life? Surely, few could fail to identify with the tale of Tim "Ripper" Owens who experienced this unlikely transformation from Mock Star to Rock Star when Rob Halford left Judas Priest during the early 1990s to work on other projects resulting in a lengthy hiatus for the band. Owens, a multi-octave vocalist and frontman of Judas Priest tribute, British Steel, was spotted by friends of the original band who alerted them to his potential as a replacement. An audition was scheduled and, after singing only one verse of the classic anthem *Victim of Changes*, he was offered the job.[4] Those weary of tales of instant celebrity, can derive comfort from the fact that the traffic from obscurity to celebrity flows in both directions. Some artists have taken the alternative route from a highlife of fame and fortune, back to the relative anonymity of the local live music scene. Prior to his untimely death in 2007 Brad Delp, lead singer of legendary 1970s rock band Boston, had forged a second career as a tribute artist in the band Beatle Juice.[5] The collective impact of stories like these when added to the karaoke craze and games like SingStar and Guitar Hero which allow you to sing like your favourite icon or play alongside them, suggests that the "mockstar" phenomenon is no longer a cultural pursuit restricted to the minority.[6]

Perhaps, more than anything, the popularity of tributes and amateur talent shows, remind us that record production is but a small part of a much bigger entertainment industry, a point reinforced by Shuker (2008: 14) who suggests that: "There is a tendency, especially in general discourse, to equate the 'music industry' with the sound recording companies, who develop and market artists and their 'records' in various format." The live sector in particular, is often overlooked and yet the popularity of tribute bands simply highlights the importance of this area of the industry. In fact, as one source puts it:

> The recorded music industry is the engine helping to drive a much broader music sector, which is worth more than US$100 billion globally. This is over three times the value of the recorded music market and shows music to have an economic impact that extends far beyond the scope of record sales. (International Federation of the Phonographic Industries, 2006)

While the major conglomerates clearly have tremendous power, their capacity to manipulate and create audiences in the less corporate world constituting the amateur and semi-professional end of the live entertainment industry, is more limited. In order to maximize profit, the preferred organization of production and consumption demands careful control of each stage, but while the record industry is relatively easy to police, the consumption of live music and the behaviour of its associated audiences are less easy to monitor.

Tribute bands are of interest particularly due to their capacity to disrupt the status quo. By returning music back to the live arena, they reverse the natural order of post-war popular music which moves traditionally, from oral performance towards notation and storage. In doing so, they remind us of the medium's social function and its capacity to generate collective behaviours capable of transcending the limitations of individual participation with recorded music. Furthermore, in an era characterized by massive innovation in the technology designed to transmit recorded music, they go against the grain by signalling a return to the low-tech and local live event. Despite the fact that digital technology has made most types of music so much more accessible, there are rising levels of dissatisfaction with the recorded medium. With the advent of the bespoke personal music collections, the whole idea of shopping for records and collecting CDs is challenged, both at the fundamental level of personal choice (you no longer have to tolerate those album tracks you hated) and more worryingly, at an economic level, where the worth of the physical product is seriously undermined. The fact that the industry continues to maintain the high prices of CDs has only fuelled illicit recording of music and the disenchantment of consumers. Bootleggers are regularly taken to court but key questions regarding the relative value of recorded music remain unanswered.

Pessimists point to the decline of the music industry in a post-digital age but on a more positive note, Kusek and Leonhard (2005: 35) suggest that, despite a growing dissatisfaction with CDs, in the wake of the digital revolution, more music than ever before is now being consumed. With downloading, legal and otherwise, music lovers have access to a far greater range of genres and artists than was ever possible in the past. Another unexpected consequence of the digital shake-up is an increase in the value attached to the scarcer commodity – live performance. Perhaps the fact that no two performances can ever be quite the same has helped to raise the status of live music as a unique product for those suffering download fatigue. It may be the case that record sales will continue to dwindle but music publishing, touring and ancillary sales remain very healthy. Renewed interest in live music has undoubtedly had an impact on the growth of the tribute entertainment industry. Furthermore, fans are more aware of to the tribute concept due to their increased awareness of the history of post-war popular music because access to the internet has ignited interest in artists and genres which might otherwise have become increasingly esoteric or even extinct.

The ascendance of the tribute is understandable when so many of us have problems distinguishing between the definitive and the copy in a cultural climate which so clearly exemplifies a Baudrillardian world of simulations and hyperreality. This is particularly true in classic rock and pop music where, as time has elapsed, the once clear distinctions between original and fake have become increasingly blurred – even more so with the regular reconfigurations of original bands which make it difficult to establish the authoritative model. If we look for example, at the current line up of the legendary Beach Boys, only one member of the original group, Mike Love, is a member. Following the death of Carl Wilson in 1998, the surviving members of the band split up into the three different tours with Brian Wilson performing alongside an eponymous band whereas Al Jardine features in two ensembles: the Endless Summer Band and the Al Jardine Family & Friends Beach Band (which confusingly features his sons Matt and Adam and Brian Wilson's daughters Wendy and Carnie). Just to confound us further, in 2007 Wilson and Jardine joined forces to undertake a European Tour!

Amidst all this confusion, is it any wonder some of us hark back to times past when there was less uncertainty and the big name rock bands were recognizable entities? Or does something more dysfunctional lie behind our desire to relive the music of our youth and are we simply doomed to be victims of a seemingly endless wave of nostalgia? The unrelenting appetite for the past provides at least a partial explanation for the tributes to deceased or defunct members of the rock pantheon but what about the proliferation of bands which pay tribute to successful current rock and pop outfits? Surely, this must be yet another example of end stage capitalism where "stylistic innovation is no longer possible" and "all that is left is to imitate dead styles" (Jameson 1983: 115). Of course, a lot depends on whether or not you are able to appreciate the positive aspect of the phenomenon. The recycling of dead styles rattles the philosopher's cage but there is clearly an over-supply of competent musicians out there and it could be argued that tribute bands acts are correcting the disequilibrium by providing work in a growth industry. Furthermore, while their proliferation can be attributed to specific factors, such as the exigencies of time, where an original group has disbanded or someone has died and the primary band no longer performs live, their ability to resurrect the repertoire enables fans to enjoy a live experience which might otherwise be lost forever.

This book aims to challenge the view of cultural pessimists by looking at tributes with a fresh eye, giving credit to a form of entertainment which needs to be understood within a wider historical context of similar and related developments in the culture of popular music. It seeks to understand the phenomenon less as a failure to achieve an unrealistic goal of unfettered "originality" and more as an example of a rich and varied tradition of live music and performance. By looking at how groups are formed, why musicians enter this area of work in the first place, and how careers are initiated and sustained in what is a without question, a cut-throat industry, I try to give a realistic account of what it is like to earn a living out of paying homage. Mindful of Howard Devoto's argument that: "Some will pay for what others pay to avoid," the book seeks the opinions and reflections of practitioners and the fans of tributes to counter those of the critics.[7] Following Zuben's (2001: 5) view that imitative practice, "is not merely a world of simulation, simulacra, and blank parody, but involves an aesthetics of engagement, self-definition, collective practice and desire," I attempt to recount the individual nuances of tribute entertainment through an study of the aforementioned qualities and practices, in an exploration of a scene capable of performing everything: from the past and the present, to the "what might have been."[8]

2 Tribute Bands in Context

Before considering the history of the tribute band, some contextual background will offer an explanation for their appearance on the music scene during the late 1970s. Factors underpinning their existence can be divided into technological and cultural developments, with technology in particular making possible the detailed study needed to carry out credible imitation. Design innovation led to the new types of equipment needed to reproduce studio engineered music within a live setting while developments in digital technology allowed musicians to market and manage themselves at relatively low cost, the latter development being an important factor for those operating on a modest budget. Finally, the internet opened up a valuable communication channel between artists and audience, a major consideration in such a fan-led branch of entertainment. Without these developments it is unlikely that the phenomenon in its present form, would have been either technically or economically viable. As regards the cultural factors determining a sympathetic environment: demographic changes, the postmodern enthusiasm for nostalgia and parody, and a growing interest in rock and pop heritage have all played a part. Lastly and paradoxically, the freedom of access created by digitization and downloading has led to renewed enthusiasm and respect for real time entertainment.

The Hegemony of Modernism

Rather than asking why tribute acts surfaced when they did, it is probably more instructive to spend time considering why they didn't appear a lot earlier. As a form of entertainment they offer excellent potential to extend the life of an existing product, without necessitating a tremendous amount of investment. In the music industry, establishing a new act involves considerable risk, whereas the tried and trusted commodity is far less risky. Taking these factors into account, it is difficult to fathom why the concept was so slow in gaining acceptance. One of the most compelling reasons may be the pre-eminence of modernist ideology in the early years of popular music. The practice of retrospection utterly contradicts the forward-looking meta-narrative which defined rock and pop as from the outset, this was music to be played by the young for the young and an ageing, nostalgia-ridden fan base was never envisioned. As Owram writes in a study of the baby boomers:

> Here was a group with so much confidence in itself, with so many idealistic expectations, with so much impatience in its rhetoric that it denied the force of history. For the boomers, the past simply had to give way to the future. (Owram 1997: x)

The ideology of youth was deeply entrenched within music's raison d'être, informing not just the lyrics and sounds, but the fashion sensibilities and performance styles as well. The Who's frantic, Methedrine fuelled anthem, *My Generation*, for example, professes a preference for death over dotage. Its arrogant ageist stance, heightened by lead vocalist Roger Daltrey's deliberately inarticulate, faux-teenage stuttering, sums up the mood of youthful angst and rebellion. There is certainly an incongruity between the lyrics, performance style and attitude of most of the youth-oriented output of the 1960s and the whole notion of "serious" homage. Nevertheless, two decades later, equipped with a vast repertoire and more statesmanlike demeanour, the icons of rock and pop were ready to don the mantle of maturity – not to mention any concomitant financial rewards to be garnered from tributes and re-releases.[1]

Playing With the Past: Music Heritage as Product

After a relatively slow start, the practice of paying tribute grew in popularity and nowadays, honouring the past has become one of the most lucrative aspects of an industry progressively defined by its own halcyon days. Media executives take full advantage of the retrospective turn to fulfil corporate goals, and, "the logic of the music industry [which] determines that recycling, repackaging, remixing and revivalism allow corporations to sell the same produce again and again" (Zuberi 2001: 5). What led to this apparent volte-face? The about turn can be traced back to the closing years of the 1960s. Although optimism in post-war popular culture was conflated with a rejection of the past, disillusion with the modernist dream did eventually give way to more recollective sensibilities. British artists and designers, inspired by major exhibitions of the work of nineteenth-century artists and designers were among the first to reacquaint themselves with the past, but interest quickly spread elsewhere, igniting a desire for the recherché. Before long, retro-clothing, furniture, prints and accessories were all embraced by the young and fashionable in a nostalgic mood captured by the novelist Angela Carter, who writes of the metropolitan fascination for, "Second hand furniture, old houses, old clothes" and "those vast, whitewashed rooms with bare floorboards and a mattress in the corner with an Indian coverlet."[2]

In Huyssen's (1986: 16) opinion, the popular culture industries were pivotal in communicating the retrocentric Zeitgeist. He suggests that, "Pop in the broadest sense was the context in which a notion of the postmodern first took shape," and certainly by the late 1970s the Teddy Boy, Mod, 2-Tone and Ska revivals epitomize the mood of an era informed, defined even, by backward looking sensibilities. Critics have a tendency to pathologize these excursions into the past, berating the apparent loss of faith in the present: Jameson (1988: 198) for instance, is particularly scathing complaining that: "Today, we cannot focus our own present, as though we have become incapable of achieving aesthetic representation of our current experience" and "if that is so, it is a terrible indictment of consumer capitalism." Although his remarks conflate nostalgia with the economics of contemporary culture, it is worth noting that the tendency to revisit the past for inspiration is by no means restricted to postmodern times. Even more obsessed with the past, were the Victorians – notably in the fields of architecture and fashion, where contemporary designers sought inspiration through an eclectic investigation of diverse and disparate historical periods. The classical and medieval styled public buildings in Victorian cities are monuments to their desire to bring to life, the visual signifiers of a lost era. Their presence embodies a mindset of resistance to the dehumanizing effects of standardization where the revival of Gothic and Classical style represented a retreat from the present.

The motivation of the Victorians, can at least be linked to an overall dissatisfaction with modern values and aesthetics, and whilst this may have a bearing on the twenty-first-century flight from the present, contemporary society's unhealthy fear of ageing must also be implicated. We live in an era where refusal to submit to the passage of time is a compelling leitmotif. From reality television programmes such as ABC's *Extreme Makeover* and the Channel 4 series *Ten Years Younger*, to magazines and newspaper features on the best way to stay young, anything which responds to our desire to prolong youth is welcomed. In this ageist environment any entertainment capable of transporting us to our youth, resonates with the cultural mood. By recapturing the look and sound of our collective past, the tribute act, offers a much needed refuge from temporal constraints.

Nostalgia in Context

Particularly susceptible to the forces of nostalgia and the desire to remain young, are those born around and immediately after the Second World War. This demographic is keenly committed to reliving their past, and with good reason. They were after all, the first generation to enjoy the experience of a cultural climate dedicated to youth and youth consumerism. Now, in terms of their "silver" spending power, they are an attractive consumer group particularly since they refuse to let go of their youthful obsession with popular music.

As Negus (2001: 68) writes: "The teenagers of the 1950s and youth of the 1960s who grew up with the record buying habit are becoming an expanding market of middle-aged pop consumers." His observations are backed up by Hull's (2004) study of changing trends in the recording industry where research findings shows the extent to which the age profile of consumers has changed. Over a 12 year period, a subtle initial shift eventually gives way to a demographic sea change.

> In 1990, over 42 percent of the consumers were under age 25 and just 20 percent over age 40. By 1995 the under-25 group had dropped to 40 percent and the 40-and-over group had grown to 24.4 per cent. By 2002 the change was even more dramatic, with the under-25 group only consuming 33.7 per cent of recording sold while the 40-and-over group had surpassed them with 35.4 per cent of sales. (Hull 2004: 8)

Now that popular music no longer belongs exclusively, as it once did, to the young, the over-40s category are the marketing executives' dream demographic: estimates suggest that in the UK they are currently responsible for almost 80 per cent of all financial wealth, and 30 per cent of consumer spending (Carrigan and Szmigin 2000). In their determination to resist the passage of time, much of their collective spending power is devoted to the extension of youth.

> As a generation, the baby boomers are ... [rejecting] many of the traditional associations of old age. In making personal fulfilment after 50 their priority, the research shows that many will use their purchasing power, connections and self-awareness increasingly to dominate the images and rituals of popular culture. (Harkin and Huber 2004: 13)

This economic power and influence is likely to resonate for the foreseeable future and certainly for the time being, their values will continue to monopolize the popular cultural terrain. In Harkin and Huber's (2004: 13) opinion: "From middle-aged men and women on motorbikes to new beauty products and treatments and music retailing, the dominance of baby boomers and their own formative icons will only grow."

Not only are the oldies hanging on like grim death to the music and fashion of their youth, they are equally determined to influence their children and grandchildren's musical tastes. During the 1960s, no self-respecting teenager would listen to their parent's music, but many young people growing up in the boomers' shadow, have such a limited perception of a distinctive youth culture of their own, they fail to challenge the status quo. Festival and concert audiences reflect these changes and nowadays, it is not unusual to see representatives from all age groups at events originally aimed solely at the young. Indeed, in 2007, Glastonbury festival organizer Michael Eavis went so far as to blame the poor turnout at the festival on a growing influx of oldies, claiming that the event was becoming "too middle-aged" and "respectable" for younger festival-goers (Phillips 2007).

Widening the Parameters of Youth

Regardless of whether the omnipresence of baby boomers has diminished the youthful festival-going audience, the combined force of nostalgia and the widening of the parameters of the cultural category of "youth" has created a substantial inter-generational consumer group. Kearney (2004) proposes that nowadays, "youth" is associated more with lifestyle and attitude than it is with age, moreover, the conceptual category is used by manufacturers and marketing professionals to address the broadest possible audience and aiming products:

> not just at teenagers, but also pre-teens, who are encouraged by the market to buy commodities produced for older consumers, as well as many adults, who, despite their age, are encouraged by the market to think, act, look and, most importantly, shop as if they were young. (Kearney 2004: 2276)

The re-branding of youth allows homages to artists, genres and decades of the past, to co-exist comfortably alongside the more contemporary product. In this context, the tribute's capacity to offer live embodiment of music, past and current, is a welcome adjunct.

Reactions to the commodification of vintage popular music however, are mixed. For some observers, the recycling of pop and rock's past pages is inevitable. Cooper (2005: 229) for example, feels we should welcome the process: "As the rock era passes its 50th anniversary, reflections on both its startling influence and its remarkable longevity should be anticipated," but other writers are less philosophical, repelled even, by the very idea of purveying rock beyond its sell-by date. Music journalist John Strausbaugh (2001: 26) vetoes the notion of ageing rock stars and fans in no uncertain terms:

> Rock music simply should not be played by 55-year-old men, pretending still to be excited about playing songs they wrote 30 or 35 years ago and have played some thousands of times since. Its prime audience should not be middle-aged, balding, jelly-bellied dads who've brought along their wives and kids.

The demise of popular music's existential function clearly perturbs some critics but audiences remain resolute in their determination to disregard the gatekeepers. Fans clearly enjoy experiencing music from pop's past pages, and if this involves being entertained by the likes of Proxy Music or The Ex Pistols, so be it!

Music, Heritage and the Museum

Liberated from the role of defining and communicating youthful angst, popular music has multiple applications outside the mainstream music industry. It feeds directly into the burgeoning heritage industry, where retrospective music events are just one of the multitude of modern enterprises geared around the business of celebrating yesteryear. Almost every town and city contains either a museum, heritage centre or site of historical interest, and some can boast several. Complaining about the pervasiveness of the past and the "creeping heritage" now dominating the US, Lowenthal (1985: xv) was moved to conclude that, where once this had been limited to a handful of museums and antique shops, "the trappings of history now festoon the whole country." Dedicated to every conceivable cultural artefact and social practice, the retro-industries do appear to be multiplying at an alarming rate. According to one study (Richter 2004), between 1968 and 1987, the number of registered historical sites in the US rose from a meagre 1,200 to around 37,000, while the UK boasts an extraordinary 500,000 historical buildings and 12,000 museums.

Inevitably, since music itself, is of major cultural significance, a good deal of interest is centred on *its* heritage potential. Furthermore, as Connell and Gibson (2002) contend, popular music's spatial contexts allow it to be linked to particular geographical sites – The Rock and Roll Hall of Fame and Museum in Ohio and Graceland, the Memphis home of Elvis Presley, are two such examples. Some measure of their respective popularity includes the former's ticket sales averaging $4.2 per year and the estimated number of 268,000 visitors who made the pilgrimage to Graceland over a six month period during 2005 (Malone 2008).

Official rock tours also fit seamlessly into the heritage industry. In the UK for instance, Manchester relies very heavily on its musical past in the marketing of a modern identity – visitors to the city are nowadays offered a variety of tours which celebrate the conurbation's unique contribution to popular music.[3] Within any convergence of music, heritage and tourism, tribute acts have much to offer. Cohen (2005), notes the important role they play in promoting Liverpool's tourist attractions, especially during the annual Beatles' Week. The event, aimed at fans (especially those from outside the UK), incorporates everything from exhibitions and sales of memorabilia to performance events and competitions. Visitors from around the world descend upon the city and make their way to the epicentre of Merseybeat history, where they may enjoy a nostalgia-themed extravaganza, centred around the life and work of the Fab Four.[4]

In another powerful example of international rock heritage, Thin Lizzy fans undertake an annual pilgrimage to Ireland to celebrate the life and work of the late Phil Lynott. Although Lynott died in 1986, fans continue to pay their respects, whether at the Annual "Dedication in Dumfries" festival in Scotland or the Dublin based "Vibe for Philo" celebration.[5] At events like these, the tribute act provides a valuable physical repository for the emotional outpourings of fans and, in some cases, audiences can exceed those drawn by many an original act. The scale and success of the "Vibe" is described here by a local journalist:

> 8,000 fans paid their respect to one of Ireland's first rock stars by snapping up the merchandise and singing along fervently to their favourite Thin Lizzy ballads such as Whiskey in the Jar. Just 30 minutes after the doors opened the event T-shirts were sold out. One Japanese devotee bought £160 worth of band accessories according to the assistant manager of Irish Merchandising Services. (Haughey 1996)

Parodic entertainers have also begun to make inroads into the music festival scene where they now feature alongside high profile original acts. Their ability to perform contemporary or vintage music, when combined with the fact that they also offer very good value for money, ensures that they attract the widest possible audience. Pink Fraud played Glastonbury in 2007, Bjorn Again were on the roster for 2009 and the inclusion of Lez Zeppelin at the Bonnaroo Festival in Tennessee (2008) caused a stir when fans assumed that they were the bona fide Led Zeppelin.[6] There is even a new breed of festivals, dedicated exclusively to the art of parody. At the UK's annual Glastonbudget festival, an array of tribute acts cover the key musical moments of the 1960s–2000s. Now in its seventh year, the event is firmly established on the Spring festival scene, drawing visitors from across Europe and beyond. The successful format has been copied elsewhere, embedding the parodic festival model more firmly within the live music scene.[7]

Popular Music's Visual Turn

Pop festivals allow fans to indulge in the twin pleasures of seeing and being seen and certainly, in terms of its significance, the visual dimension of music has grown apace. Durant (1984), acknowledging the importance of the image, argues that whilst primarily an aural medium, music has always been experienced via the pleasurable act of looking. The growth of look-alike entertainment suggests that in the battle of the senses, the visual is nowadays victorious. Reiterating the point, Debord (quoted in Knabb 1981: 307), claims that we are living in a state of false consciousness, "drugged by spectacular images," while Kaplan (1987: 44) speaks of: "The new postmodern universe, with its celebration of the look – the surfaces, textures, the self-as-commodity – [which] threatens to reduce everything to the image/representation/simulacrum." It seems then, that the inflated value of the visual is symptomatic of a broader cultural shift towards the commodification of imagery, something which increasingly constitutes our sense of reality. As a result, where at one time, fans were prepared to make do with listening to records, reading about stars in the monochrome pages of the pop press and pinning grainy photographs of them onto their bedroom walls, these simpler pleasures no longer suffice. We want to consume music from our collective pasts which not only sounds authentic but also *looks* right. Within this voyeuristic climate, the stature and earning capacity of the look-alike tribute band far exceeds than that of its more innocent predecessor – the cover band.

Acceptance of the Fake Article

Attitudes to faking have also undergone major revision. In the past, the fake article was shunned but in many quarters, phony goods and forgeries are now accepted – admired even – as is the art of copying itself. Inspired by the delights of deception, in a study of museums, galleries and other tourist attractions in the US, Umberto Eco (1986) invites readers to join him on his excursions to works of fake genius such as a full reproduction of the president's Oval Office at the White House, a wax statue of the Mona Lisa and a "restored" copy of the Venus de Milo (complete with arms). His pilgrimage into the world of the hyperreal led him to the revelation that the imitations he encountered not only reproduced reality, but improved upon it! Although Benjamin (1973a: 220) made a spirited defence of the qualities of the original, arguing that, "Even the most perfect reproduction of a work of art is lacking in one element: its presence in time and space, its unique existence at the place where it happens to be," Eco's research is important because it shows that admiration for the special aura associated with the original has given way to a frank appreciation of fakery. Thus, we are happy to pay more for look-alikes because we choose to be deceived by their artful illusion.

Arguments concerning the special character of the original are increasingly hard to sustain anyway with regards to popular music, where technology has created a host of new complexities. As Goodwin (1988) points out, it is particularly difficult to speak of originality post-"sampling," citing the example of the hit single *Pump Up The Volume*, a record which makes use of fragments taken from 30 others. The fact that sampling is acceptable at all illustrates the widespread acceptance of pastiche and theft. Witness too, the elevated status of art forgers such as Tom Keating, who in his lifetime claims to have faked over two thousand paintings by over one hundred world famous artists. Even on a personal level copying is becoming more acceptable since the average consumer is surprisingly approving of fake products.[8] According to a Mori poll commissioned by the UK's Anti-Counterfeiting Group (ACG), a third of Brits said that they would "knowingly purchase counterfeit goods if the price and quality of goods was right" (Sherwood 2003). In a cultural climate which embraces the studied imitation and fake designer products, the artfully contrived tribute is a welcome development – fakes are no longer second-rate, they are positively fashionable.

The Rise of Retro-Retailing

Without the appropriate paraphernalia, the retro-illusion would be insufficiently convincing and if entertainers are to provide a suitably authentic copy, they are dependent on the availability of essential tools of the trade. These are supplied by the nostalgia-oriented business sector, an army of retailers who specialize in second-hand goods and reproductions, a market sector which has expanded significantly over the past 40 years. Gregson, and Crewe (2003: 21–25) link the proliferation of second-hand sales to a noticeable growth in demand. Alongside an increase in the number of car boot sales and charity shops, they point to the growing sophistication of retro-retailers who sell period clothing and memorabilia. Although most of these businesses currently exist within an economic "third space" of market stalls and short-lease shopping units there are also clusters of traders operating in the more fashionable neighbourhoods of major cities.[9]

Beatlesuits.com, a company established by an entrepreneur who gave up selling sportswear in order to clothe the burgeoning legion of Beatles' tributes, provides a useful case study for the new breed of retro-retailers.[10] Owner Russ Lease was an avid collector of Beatles' memorabilia and spent 30 years trawling auction rooms, where he acquired a number of outfits worn by original band members. Unsure as to how he might use them to make a living, he describes the epiphany moment:

> I was kind of pushed into it by some tribute band people that I knew. The bands who would replicate The Beatles' show really had a hard time coming up with the outfits. What they would do is go to the

> Salvation Army and consignment shops and buy older, used clothing suits and try to find things from the 60s and 70s. They would buy them and take them to tailors and have them change this lapel and lengthen this cuff and take it in here and try to make it look as English as possible. But, they really never had a place to go where they could buy something off the rack that was an exact copy of some of those early and mid 60s styles. I think that sort of pushed me into it. (Gary James, "Interview With Beatles' Memorabilia Collector Russ Lease," www.classicbands.com/RussLeaseInterview.html)

Clearly a wise move! Now a profitable enterprise, the shop offers a wide selection of outfits which includes the collarless suits of early 1960s, the Nehru style jackets worn at Shea Stadium, a "Hard Days Night Suit" and the "Crosswalk Jacket" worn by Ringo Starr on the cover of the *Abbey Road* album (Figure 2.1). The shop also stocks other must-have items such as replicas of the *Sgt. Pepper* drumhead and the star shaped "Shea" badges, presented to the band prior to the Shea Stadium concert (Figure 2.2).With a turnover of $200,000 on Beatles' outfits alone, the business is expanding to profit further from the past by widening its portfolio to include replicas of the wardrobes of other iconic 1960s bands.

Figure 2.1 "Crosswalk" jacket (photograph Russ Lease, by permission)

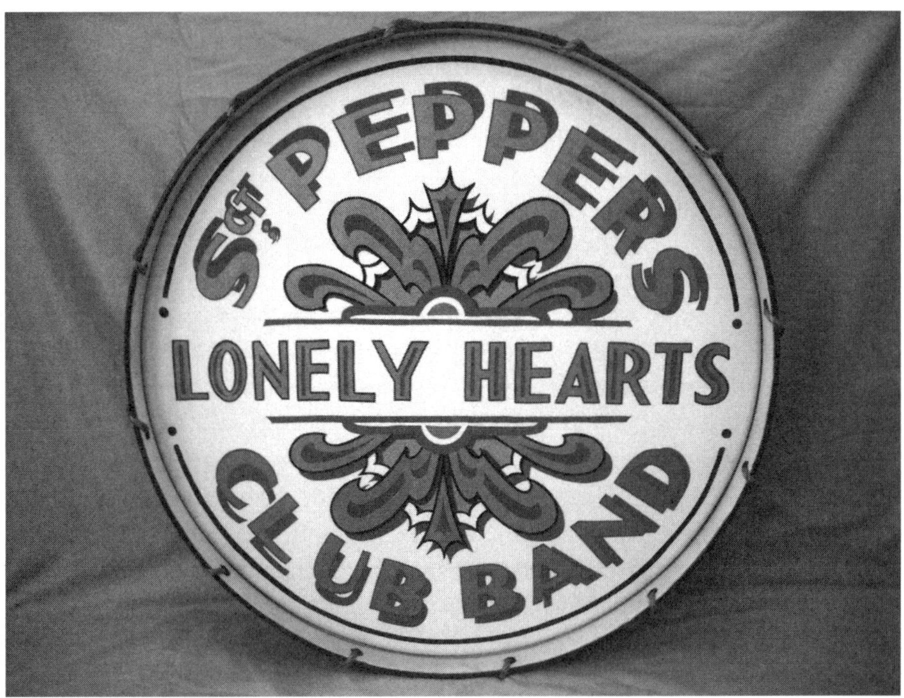

Figure 2.2 Sgt. Pepper drumhead (photograph Russ Lease, by permission)

New Instruments – New Technology

Without the appropriate technology it is very unlikely that the tribute band phenomenon would have happened, but then Holmes (2002) argues, without the benefits of modern technology, popular music as we know it today would not exist for, as Frith (1990: 141) writes: "The introduction of music industry technology inevitably affects the way music is performed and the people who perform it." For those performing in tribute acts, developments like video and music television made possible the detailed study needed to give a credible simulation of repertoire and performance. The wider availability of instruments and equipment enabled amateur and semi-professional musicians to establish themselves in ways which would have been unthinkable during the 1960s.

If we look first at the essential tools of the trade, instruments and equipment, imitative entertainers are reliant on a complex combination of the old and new. Fans expect to see original instruments so parodic entertainers may need to invest in these. However, alongside any period instruments they have acquired, bands will usually be in possession of a veritable arsenal of state-of-the-art equipment including anything from elaborate PA systems, mixers, amplifiers, Korg and Roland synthesizers to drum pads and vocoders.

Digital samplers which can store multiple recordings within the equipment's memory, are particularly useful. These recordings can be accessed rapidly and played back to replicate the sound of vintage instruments. The Ensonique Performance Sampler (EPS) is just one example of this new generation of technological tools, allowing musicians to have several instruments on line at once with the possibility of switching between them – an important innovation for anyone charged with the rigours of entertaining live, where performance must not be restricted by too many physical limitations. Samplers allow tribute artists to deliver the more complicated productions recorded by artists such as The Beatles and The Beach Boys whose complex arrangements and recording techniques would otherwise defy live performance.

Although new technology makes some original instruments optional, artists will still go to great lengths to acquire authentic vintage kit and intense competition places a premium on scarce gear. Confirming previous observations on the importance attached to the spectacle, the quest for the authentic is fuelled more by a concern for visual authenticity than it is by a desire to authenticate sound reproduction. A member of staff at one US vintage equipment store explains:

> In my business, tribute bands often tend to require the exact make and model of every piece of gear that was used by the original band. This will cause a surge in demand for certain items that previously were of little or no interest, thus driving the market value of those items to astronomical levels. Another interesting point is that there are often comparable pieces of gear from the same era that will get the same sound and do the same job, maybe even better. Yet the prices of those similar items will remain stable. Case in point – due to the number of U2 tribute bands, the price of a vintage Korg SDD-3000 is up over $1000.00, whereas the Roland SDE-3000 (a comparable effect that can more or less serve the same purpose) can be had for less than half the price. (Tom H. of the Analogue team at For Musicians Only, interview, March, 2008)

One thousand dollars for a synthesizer may seem a hefty price tag but equipment today is far more affordable than it was during the early years of rock and pop. According to Theberge (1997) the relative affordability of equipment is a major factor in the democratization of popular music practice. Where once, only the professionals could afford to purchase good quality equipment, lower prices have eroded the distinction between professional and amateur musicians, enabling everyone from the semi-professional to the "weekend warrior" to break into music making.

Communicating with Digital Technology

The impact of arrival of the internet on communication should not be underestimated. Some indication of its significance can be gleaned from the following extract of a survey which illustrates the dramatic spread of new media into small to medium sized businesses (SMEs).

> Digital technologies are becoming all pervasive across the music SMEs surveyed, more so than for SMEs in general. 85% of the music businesses have a website and 53% of those with a website are engaged in e-commerce, compared with 60% and 13% respectively for all SMEs. (Department of Culture, Media and Sport (2006) SME Music Businesses: Business Growth and Access to Finance).

Pre-internet: promotion, marketing and associated administration was relatively expensive and time consuming, as a member of The Counterfeit Kinks recounts.

> Initially when we started (1990/91), any fan base was supported by the use of paper-only methods – mail outs by Royal Mail, and paper flyers handed out prior to, or after shows to offer information about forthcoming shows, or request people to write to us. (Wayne McAneaney, interview, March 2009)

Multi-platform digital technology makes day-to-day communication easier, cheaper and more effective, an important consideration for tribute acts as most do not have the same degree of professional support as signed artists. Turow (2008: 401) found that most bands now use a combination of bespoke websites, file sharing channels and social networking sites and expansion of the internet makes it easier for them to contact agents, promoters and venues. Internet technology facilitates networking with other musicians and most importantly, it provides instant access to fans, enabling artists to communicate directly with the audience. At minimal cost, the Web can be used to offer biographical information, blogs, band histories, MP3s as well as details regarding forthcoming gigs and merchandise. Musicians can use digital media as a tool to monitor popularity and develop camaraderie, loyalty and rapport with the audience while fans may use it to create a dialogue with the performers and co-fans. Ash Brookes, the "Paul Stanley" of KISS tribute, Dressed to Kill, describes the impact of the internet on his group's marketing strategies:

> When the internet was starting to open out, we still had to rely on paper based methods of advertising to our fans with some of the more "affluent" members (a minority) having access to PCs and then

> the net, enabling us to email them. The availability of internet access then began to widen and so did our fanbase (via email). Webforums were becoming even more popular as net access generally had become more widely available, especially via PCs at workplaces. The inception of social networking sites has affected perception of us in a most positive way, and has been instrumental in our increasing audience. We market and promote via MySpace and Facebook almost exclusively – and exploit the zero cost "advertising" thereon – and on national/international (demographic specific) webforums such as *Kerrang, Metal Hammer* etc. (Ash Brookes, email, March 2009)

Since accurate detail is essential for success, this too is assisted by access to the web and without doubt the growth of imitative entertainment relates to the wider availability of good quality research tools. Successive developments in media technology are allowing would-be performers access to the sources needed for the creation of a credible tribute. Before music television and the internet, the process was a challenge but with the appropriate "tools of the trade" historical performances can be studied repeatedly to observe everything from, mannerisms and stage banter to the organization of repertoire, costumes, period instruments, pyrotechnics and other visual effects. Lyrics and tablatures are also freely available online and agents, equipment and instruments are easy to source.

According to Burns' (1996: 132) music television and pop video were primary vehicles in the mobilization of an accessible pop and rock history. In this respect VH1 (Video Hits One), MTV's station aimed at the older viewer, was particularly influential, paving the way for a wave of programming geared around recycling the sound and images of the 1960s–1990s. With the arrival of YouTube it is easy for all of us to dip effortlessly in and out of the past and in terms of their capacity to augment our awareness of pop music's past, the vast catalogue of "rockumentaries" documenting everything from the collective culture of post-war youth, to the work and lives of iconic artists, provide ever more opportunities to traverse temporal boundaries. With constant exposure to the sheer number of films, websites, television and radio programmes infused with pop-historical content our awareness is heightened, as is our desire to re-live those epic moments.

One manifestation of this ahistorical brainwashing is a postmodern blurring of the boundaries between our contemporary and youthful selves. To all intents and purposes, the past is no longer the proverbial "foreign country" where people do things differently. Instead, it has become a regular destination for youthful cultural tourists and born again teenagers keen to experience past popular music and youthful affect. Courtesy of YouTube for example, it is possible for fans to relive the excitement of The Beatles' 1964 concert at Shea Stadium while Beatles tributes, in reflexive intertextual mode, can make use of the same text to present their own versions of the epic concert.[11] In such a retrocentric environment, the tribute band can only thrive.

Live Music – Post Digital

Paradoxically, new technology has inflated the value of live music but then, as Kusek and Gerd (2005) remind us, the record industry is only one of many aspects of a much larger enterprise and for the download generation, CDs are becoming a less attractive option, driving them to consider alternative options for leisure and pleasure. For some, a visit to the live event is an increasingly appealing choice, and according to one report this is a worldwide trend. Andrew (2009) writes that, "The turnover of the global live music sector rose by 10 per cent in 2008 to more than $25bn, while the global retail value of recorded music sales fell by 7 per cent to $26.5bn." Other research indicates that touring is back in fashion and revenues from this income stream are also on the increase – the recent tours of Take That, Bruce Springsteen and Madonna amongst others, are a testimony to demand for seasoned live performers.[12]

Where record players and transistor radios used to be located firmly in the home, renewed interest in live music signals the medium's return to the public sphere by reversing the post-war drift towards domestication (Shuker 1994: 55). Portable products could never replace the intimacy of live music or the immediacy and excitement of the pop or rock concert anyway, and the popularity of tributes shows that despite advances in home technology fans still want to feel music – see, hear and if at all possible, touch the performers. In the smaller clubs and theatres frequented by tribute acts, their desires can be realized. As Homan (2007) points out, the ascendancy of the tribute scene can be related to disaffection with the stadium rock phenomenon and auditoriums where bands like the Stones, U2 and Led Zeppelin can command audiences of over 50,000.[13] Large scale events might make economic sense by accommodating the maximum number of fans but for many, the experience is a disappointment. The high price of tickets and refreshments when combined with the impersonal nature of the venues almost inevitably lower levels of audience satisfaction and although giant video screens attempt to widen access to performers, intimacy is inevitably sacrificed in the process of mediatization.

Smaller live venues offer qualities which the multi-media arena event can never deliver, mainly because they are able to provide an intimate atmosphere but also because of their accessibility and individual quirkiness. They may not be able to attract the megastars but what they do offer, is something many crave: an element of old-fashioned personal service and when value for money is added to the mix, it is easy to see why they are so popular. Hard data on smaller clubs is difficult to find but in the UK at least, there is evidence that live venues are enjoying something of a renaissance. According to a survey commissioned by the Department of Culture, Media and Sport (MORI: 2004), nearly half of the small clubs and bars approached had featured live acts at least once in the previous year and the majority intended to continue doing so. All this suggests that the status of live music has changed and in relation to its recorded counterpart, it is becoming the scarcer commodity. In a changing market for music, tribute acts can only continue to flourish, exploiting their capacity to respond to audience expectations in an altered consumer landscape where "small" is beautiful and the past is seamlessly integrated into the present.

3 From "Ghost" and Cover Bands, to Pop Parody and Tributes

In order to situate the contemporary pop homage in the context of related examples of revivalism and curatorship, this chapter explores musical tribute in a historical trajectory. Before going on to discuss the factors surrounding the emergence of the modern tribute act, I will look at one of the key forerunners explaining how, in the absence of their leaders, "ghost" bands, helped to keep alive the repertoire and identity of big bands. This will be followed by an evaluation of the role played by cover bands in offering music lovers live versions of chart music of the 1960s – during an era when the international tour was an infrequent event, their role as transatlantic ambassadors is explored. Consideration is also given to pop parody and impersonation – entertainment models which helped to popularize the theme of recycling identities, thereby paving the way for the fully fledged tribute acts we are all familiar with.

Paying Tribute, Past and Present

The use of the term "tribute" is significant: mainly because the art of paying tribute has much more positive associations than the potentially dishonest act of impersonation. Unlike the noble act of paying homage, impersonation has slightly seedy connotations, linking it to criminal activity and low-brow entertainment. Any attempt to uncover the origins of the act or art of paying tribute, will find that a cultural convention which can be traced back to the earliest civilizations where the word tribute stems from the Latin noun *tributum*, meaning payment. Initially, the practice was cast in terms of a financial exchange, given by one party to another as a sign of submission, allegiance or respect, whereas later the concept acquired additional connotations of duty. In the Bible, Romans were advised sternly to, "Render ... to all their dues, tribute to whom tribute is due, custom to whom custom, fear to whom fear, honour to whom honour" (Romans 13: 6-7). The term eventually evolved into its current usage where, rather than an enforced fiscal exercise or moral obligation, it describes a voluntary act, "something given, said or done as a mark of respect or admiration."[1]

In contemporary culture, we pay tribute because we choose to validate the lives and works of those we admire in a wide variety of ways.

Within the arts where the practice is firmly entrenched, depending on the circumstances, the tone is typically commemorative, deferential, curatorial or celebratory. Speeches, memorial services, broadcast events, exhibitions and concerts are typical vehicles, but regardless of the approach chosen, in its nobler manifestations, the aim of paying tribute is to acknowledge significance or show appreciation. It would however, be disingenuous to ignore the fact that increasingly, paying homage has become a lucrative aspect of the music industry. A variety of media can be used: from the audio and visual platforms of radio, records and television, to live multimedia events. Typical themes include marking the output of a distinguished songwriter or performing artist or the career of a deceased star. Indeed, as a popular excuse for an outpouring, untimely demise is routinely addressed, by a plethora of products: from lavish boxed sets of CDs, to television documentaries and memorial concerts. Nowadays, with the introduction of computer generated imagery, death doesn't necessarily need to extinguish the production process, because physical presence can be simulated for a range of profitable purposes. In 2005 the *Notorious B.I.G. Duets* paired the murdered rap star alongside high profile living hip-hop artists such as Jay-Z, Mary J. Blige and Eminem, while the recording *Forever Cool* (2007) features the late Dean Martin crooning alongside contemporary vocal luminaries such as Robbie Williams, Charles Aznavour and Joss Stone. The digitally enhanced posthumous duet is just one example of a new means of commercial exploitation and although popular opinion is currently divided on the value of these postpartum appearances, there is every likelihood that the practice will become a regular feature of the homage industry in the future.[2]

Musical homage is also brought to play within public events, where the medium's polysemic capabilities allow it to signify everything from national identity and civic pride to general Zeitgeist. In 1999 for example, the passing of the millennium was celebrated with a collaboration between Channel 4 television, shopping giant HMV and the *The Guardian* newspaper to mark the occasion by identifying the best British music of the epoch. The ambitious survey led to a whole raft of television and radio programmes, newspaper and magazine features, all dedicated to the task of honouring popular music.[3] In addition to throwing light on the vagaries of popular taste, music was used to celebrate the historical significance of both the occasion and the passage of time. In a similar manner, at the Queen's Golden Jubilee in 2002, the decision to hold a pop concert at Buckingham Palace signalled very clearly, the importance attached to music as a signifier of British cultural identity.[4] More recently, at the inauguration of President Barak Obama in the "We Are One" celebration, American popular music was also honoured in its role as a symbol of national pride and unity. The memorable pageant featured high profile artists drawn from various sectors of the industry, illustrating music's capacity to embody the identities of America's urban and rural communities and the racial and ethnic diversity of the nation.[5]

Technology and Pop Homage

Just as technology facilitated the smooth running of the tribute scene, determining the types of instruments and means of communication on hand, it plays an equally important role in determining the character of pop tribute, with different developments, placing particular limitations and challenges on the delivery.[6] Radio for example, prohibits the visual dimension of pop and rock, thus limiting an important sensory channel and although television can deliver this aspect, its domestic setting inhibits popular music's more rebellious impulses. As Frith (1983: 153) writes: "The effect of fitting rock'n'roll into a medium like television is to make it safe, to deprive it of some of its significance," because "an undifferentiated audience can't be a rock audience."[7] Film is also handicapped by the limitations imposed by mainstream broadcasting within which, pop does not always fit very comfortably. When pop tributes do appear on screen, they are normally marshalled into those ultra-populist entertainment formats inscribed with mass audience appeal. In television for examples, programmes such as the *100 Greatest* series, invite us to reflect upon the respective merits of a pre-selected set of popular albums, singles or songs – looking at the best, the worst and just about everything in between.[8]

For various reasons records have been one of the most popular delivery formats – in terms of convenience and cost, they offer a particularly practical solution – a fact reflected in the sheer volume of albums dedicated to the task. As a tool of mass-production capable of furthering the life of a commodity, the tribute record neatly embodies the industry's consumer-oriented *raison d'être* by realizing pop's pragmatic preference for reiteration. Straw (1993) writes that the culture of popular music embraces familiarity and the enduring reverence for past hit songs ensures that they are regularly revisited. Reworking of a musical product certainly makes economic sense: prior to the advent of pop and rock, the practice of recycling songs was an accepted practice: this was especially so within the orthodoxy of jazz, where the collusion between executives and sheet music companies ensured that a limited range of popular songs were constantly reworked.

Embodying this philosophy, the tribute album is of course, an exceptionally versatile medium, creating seemingly endless possibilities to re-deploy existing texts. Albums allow individuals or groups to pay tribute to the output of fellow artists, thus optimizing the re-use of established hits and at the same time, reinforcing the importance of a limited range of canonized works. The history of the recorded tribute can be charted back to the opening years of the twentieth century, where the idea was first explored, long before the introduction of modern album technology. In 1907, the popular tenor Enrico Caruso made a recording of Leoncavallo's aria *Vesti la giubba* for Victor Records and according to Ruhlmann (2004: 12) the phonograph was a best seller, with contemporary estimates pointing to sales of over a million, a figure many contemporary artists would dearly love to achieve.

The concept of the tribute record was also embraced within the jazz genre, where interpretation of a shared repertoire is customary, since the ontology of jazz permits re-presentation of key works and attempts to interpret popular songs or melodies do not constitute "covering" in a pejorative sense. In jazz circles, tribute albums are sometimes used to introduce the work of newcomers, allowing record companies to minimize potential risk by offering audiences an element of familiarity. Tucker (1999) describes the practice in relation to iconic artist, Thelonious Monk:

> Monk – a thirty-seven-year-old pianist and composer still not widely known to the public – made his debut recording for the Riverside label, released under the title *Thelonious Monk Plays Duke Ellington.*

As he goes on to explain, the majority of the album's content was unoriginal or featured work associated with other artists:

> Monk interpreted eight compositions by the popular, internationally acclaimed Ellington. Nearly all were standards frequently performed by established singers and instrumentalists: "Sophisticated Lady," "I Got It Bad (and That Ain't Good)," "Solitude," "Mood Indigo," "It Don't Mean a Thing If It Ain't Got That Swing," "I Let a Song Go Out of My Heart," and the Ellington-Juan Tizol collaboration "Caravan." (Tucker 1999: 228)

Tribute albums were not as successfully incorporated within the culture of post-war popular music however and to some extent this was due to a conflation of artist and song which gradually came to characterize the genre. After singer/songwriters emerged during the 1960s, rock artists were expected to write and perform their own material, but this departure from the Tin Pan Alley songwriting tradition led to a less positive perception of rock and pop recordings and performances of material composed by anyone other than the author. As Straw (1999: 200) contends, when making judgements of relative merit, "we evaluate a musical recording or concert as the output of a single individual or group" and for the majority, unauthored music has less appeal.

The Failure of Low-Cost Cover Records

It is interesting to observe how the tendency to identify pop songs with specific artists relates to the long term failure of anonymous budget label cover records where public perception of the product as a second-rate option, demonstrates consumers' preference for music identified with a recognizable author. During the 1960s, the Embassy Record label, produced almost identical versions of current chart hits in a series of albums and double A-sided singles, featuring in some cases, a different artist on each side of the recording. The company emerged from a contractual agreement between Woolworth's and the Oriole Record label to supply records at far lower cost than those sold by the major labels. Notwithstanding the considerable saving they offered, or the fact that many of these recordings featured well-known musicians operating under pseudonyms, the concept was never fully embraced by fans. The product may have enjoyed limited chart success but ultimately, its value was deflated by the absence of a true star identity.[9]

If anonymity was an unattractive marketing tool in the battle to sell more records, the authored pop tribute appears to have been more successful as it was able to offer fans a recording of tried and trusted music, already identified with a well-known artist. If we look at the output of the dominant record labels, there are some examples of recorded tributes by successful pop artists, dedicated to established auteurs during the first half of the 1960s. These include folk group Peter, Paul and Mary's respectful homage to Bob Dylan in a compilation entitled, *In the Wind* (1963) and two years later, The Brothers Four released an EP of Dylan songs: *The Brothers Four Sing Bob Dylan*. Despite the fact that the records were offering new versions of the well-known material, the pop tribute didn't fully grab the popular imagination until the 1970s, by which time a body of well-known songwriters had a repertoire of established and popular music upon which to draw. Although not regarded as a shared repertoire in the time honoured jazz sense, the music was at least already accepted in critical terms. With the nostalgic turn of the 1970s the album became a fashionable vehicle for homage, as popular culture took a retrospective turn and high-profile artists followed one another in quick succession to produce albums reflecting the roots of their musical inspiration, as well as their admiration for one another. Notable examples include *Pin Ups* (1973), David Bowie's salute to the 1960s; John Lennon's (1975) tribute to the music of the 1950s, *Rock'n' Roll* and Bryan Ferry's eclectic overview of his favourite artists on the album *These Foolish Things* (1973).

Musical Revivals

Retrospective impulses may have been particularly fashionable during the 1970s but the desire to bring to life music of another era has a far lengthier pedigree. Pop tributes can be related to a much wider practice of musical revivalism, defined by ethnomusicologist Tamara Livingston (1997: 66), as a conscious undertaking to elicit interest in music which has been forgotten entirely, or in situations where interest has waned. The scope of the revival may embrace anything, from the musical output of an entire geographical area, to the revival of the use of a specific instrument or even the work of individual artists, ensembles, genres and sub-genres. At the popular end of the cultural spectrum, an historical example of this type of revivalism is provided by Booth and Kaplan (1991: 678) who, in their study of Edwardian theatre, describe the performances of the music hall diva Marjorie Dawson. As "The Crinoline Girl," Dawson delighted older members of the audience with her renditions of well-loved Victorian songs. It is interesting to note that in addition to keeping alive a repertoire of popular music, rather like some of her counterparts on the modern tribute scene, much of her appeal may be attributed to her revival of period costume and more particularly, that signature nineteenth century undergarment, the crinoline.

We should not assume however, that the shallow lure of the visual is confined solely to the world of popular entertainment since even in the loftier world of classical music, practitioners readily succumb to the demand for period instruments and clothing. Just as contemporary tribute artists strive to create an authentic performance by various means, scholars and performers of classical music, wrestle with the minutiae of accurate representation. Since techniques, instruments and performance practices change over time, it is not always easy to establish a composer's original intentions. Although classical musicians can, at least, refer to the tangible remains provided by the musical score, this too is open to interpretation. The role of unravelling the mysteries of previously performed music is left to various groups and individuals to decipher.

According to Lawson and Stowell (1999) the classical performance movement, a rather unlikely predecessor of the pop tribute, was established in the opening years of the twentieth century. In common with other revivalists, those who subscribe to the movement wrestle with particular issues regarding interpretation, many of which they struggle to resolve:

> Even if we did know the myriad details about a particular set of performances, the venue and reasons for performing music in the late twentieth century will be different to those prevailing in earlier

> times. Which compromises are tolerable, and which not, will clearly always be an area where musicians disagree. (Howard Mayer Brown 1988: 27)

They must for instance decide, whether or not to play the music in the way the composer intended, by using period instruments rather than modern copies. To this end, their concerns are very similar to those of the musicians in tribute bands who have to use their judgement when deciding between an original instrument or the contemporary copy. Though they are primarily concerned with getting the music right, certain subscribers to historical performance also take on board the sartorial aspect and opt for period costume. The critically acclaimed Mozart Festival Orchestra in their efforts to achieve a degree of authenticity, regularly performs by candlelight and musicians wear wigs and eighteenth-century costumes.[10]

Several other orchestras adopt a similar approach. Described as "one of the finest exponents of baroque music in the country" and the "original tribute band" – The 18th Century Concert Orchestra is equally committed to reviving the visual aspect as a description of one of their performances indicates.

> The scene is set by Mr Holt, our dedicated Master of Candles, providing illumination before the musicians appear in their resplendent 18th century attire. The assembled band, comprising of fiddlers, hautboys and harpsichordist, bow gracefully and soon launch into a striking overture – perhaps one of Don Antonio Vivaldi's ... Concertos, arias and dance suites are interspersed with informative and witty anecdotes drawn from 18th century histories, journals and treatises. (www.18thcentury.co.uk).

In the interests of authenticity, their painstaking simulation makes use of historically informed *mise-en-scène* such as, "period instruments, wooden music desks, individually tailored costumes and shoes, mohair wigs, candlelight and readings" (www.18thcentury.co.uk). Purists may be scornful of these theatrics, perhaps because in pandering to the lowest common denominator of sensory perception, the less cerebral aspect of performance is invoked. Nevertheless, audiences clearly welcome the added visual dimension and the critiques of the pleasure evoked by historical costume resonate with a much more widespread suspicion concerning clothing's seductive powers. This aversion to costume's potential allure, is attributed by Pamela Church Gibson (in Bruzzi and Church Gibson 2000: 265), to "the centuries old belief in the essential frivolity of fashion," a puritanical view shared by many critics who prefer to witness more intellectual forms of audience engagement.

Arguments concerning the frivolous nature of fashion are much more difficult to sustain *vis-à-vis* popular music, where style is fundamental to the genre's *raison d'être*. The theme of style and clothing has been regularly revisited in songs as varied as The Kinks' *Dedicated Follower of Fashion* (1966); *Fashion* (1980), David Bowie's ode to haute couture and, more recently, references to designer labels inform the content of numerous rap recordings. Indeed, the blatant conflation of popular music and fashion led Frith (1996: 157) to conclude, "pop is nothing if not fashionable," a point elaborated by McLaughlin (2001: 269) who says, "Rock has always depended on visual images, fashion, theatricality and spectacle," moreover he suggests that, "clothing and dress are an important aspect of how popular music functions." For these reasons, any revival of pop music invariably involves a parallel revivification of fashions associated with the genre. If we look, for example, at the UK Mod and Teddy Boy revivals of the 1970s, the fashions were just as painstakingly copied as the music and dance moves.

The concerns of critics of popular music revivals are suspiciously similar to those expressed by the detractors of the historical performance. Rather than representing curatorial skill, they see the resurrection of sounds, fashions and performance styles as exemplifying creative exiguity (Blakemore 1990). Moreover, wholesale style revivals of specific pop and rock genres, are interpreted as a worst case scenario of the postmodern drift towards reflection, pastiche and quotation which lamentably permits, "direct and explicit mixing of styles, the 'infiltration' of other genres of music in a self-conscious way, as well as the stitching together, remixing, quoting of different music, sounds or instruments" (Woods 1999: 172).

Although the apparent lack of originality may infuriate critics, it does not seem to deter audiences from deriving pleasure out of this type of re-enactment. Moreover, although the success of the tribute act is often attributed to the postmodern retrospective turn, its ability to offer the invaluable live dimension of popular music, is often overlooked. Whilst mass production has increased our access to the recording, record and CD ownership is only one aspect of the wider culture surrounding popular music. The private consumption of music cannot by itself, fulfil important social needs whereas live entertainment has the power to tap into our desire to engage with music collectively.

Successful recording artists are only too aware of the potential loss in earnings they may incur if they ignore the audience's need for a real time sensory relationship. Furthermore, the live dimension is acknowledged as an indispensable marketing tool and as Shuker (2008: 57) points out, this is the main reason why artists subject themselves to the rigours of international touring. Fans' economic and emotional investment in live events are indicative of the premium they place on the physical embodiment of music: this is especially so where, for whatever reason, corporeal access to the artist is restricted or no longer possible. The appearance of "ghost" jazz bands illustrates how, in these circumstances, fans are willing to accept a substitute.

Cultural Templates: Ghost and Parody Bands

The jazz genre established a successful model for the live musical tribute. With the advent of popular music, the big bands were greatly diminished in number, but some, having ceased to perform officially, lived on in the form of "ghost" bands. These ensembles, which took on the name and repertoire of a well-known band, were fronted by an alternative leader, often someone who already had a close connection with the archetype. Chicago music librarian and creator of the Big Band Library website, Christopher Popa, describes three examples of circumstances leading to the emergence of a spectral substitute:

> Among the earliest examples of what later became known as a "ghost band" was when saxophonist Orville Knapp was killed in a 1936 airplane accident and his widow selected veteran leader George Olsen to continue the band. But the venture lasted only until 1938, when the band broke up. Another instance was when vocalist Ella Fitzgerald was named leader of drummer Chick Webb's Orchestra, after Webb died in June 1939. However, within a very short time, Webb's name was dropped and the group became "Ella Fitzgerald and Her Famous Orchestra," which lasted until she began a solo career in 1942. Still another example was saxophonist Hal Kemp, who lost his life in a 1940 automobile crash. His band's vocalist, Art Jarrett, took over the band. (Christopher Popa, email, March 2008)

In these cases, the death of the original band leader was the catalyst for their formation. However, Popa also cites the more unusual case of a ghost band which came into being during the leader's lifetime;

> When mercurial clarinetist Artie Shaw took an unexpected break from the music business in November 1939. Shaw was the number-one band at the time, so his sidemen tried to continue under the leadership of one of Shaw's saxophonists, Georgie Auld. They were billed as "Georgie Auld and His Artie Shaw Orchestra," but without Shaw, the commercial value no longer existed and they disbanded after several months. Shaw (who gave up playing once and for all in 1954) authorized the formation of a new big band bearing his name in 1983; since he was still living, it became the only "ghost band" without a ghost, and Shaw quipped, "And I don't intend to comply." (Christopher Popa, email, March 2008)

Whereas, in popular music circles, most tribute acts choose to be referred to as such, the big bands were more reluctant to accept their "ghost" appellation. Popa illustrates how this was reflected in their failure to use the term within publicity:

> I have never seen any poster or flyer or other print advertising where the orchestra was, using those words, referred to as a "ghost band." It's always the so-and-so orchestra directed by (or led by) so-and-so. A band's press kit sometimes adds some hyperbole such as THE WORLD FAMOUS Glenn Miller Orchestra or THE ONE AND ONLY Tommy Dorsey Orchestra or THE FABULOUS Jimmy Dorsey Orchestra. Many musicians have considered the term "ghost band" derogatory; I suppose it has been used primarily by critics and reviewers, but not in promotion of the bands. (Christopher Popa, email, March, 2008)

The ownership of a ghost band's name was occasionally disputed, however, disapproval was by no means unanimous and in some cases they operated with the permission of the original artist's representatives. This occurred following Glen Miller's untimely death in an air crash when the Miller estate authorized an official Glenn Miller "ghost" band. Other band leaders were less than enthusiastic about potential reincarnation, notably Stan Kenton and Benny Goodman, who both forbade any orchestra to operate under their name.

Critical reception of the ghost bands has been mixed – like their protégés in the world of pop, there is a tendency to castigate them for copying too closely. Gabbard (2004: 239) in a study of Hollywood and African American culture, is lukewarm, arguing that playing, "note-for-note imitations of old Swing Era recordings by Glenn Miller or the Dorseys," is against the ethos of jazz (which would not normally be played exactly the same way at each performance), he goes on to complain that the handful of repertory orchestras responsible for recreating the big band sound, "succeed more in embalming the music than bringing it to life." Going to the other extreme, very strict adherence to the original text was endorsed by the son of jazz legend, Duke Ellington. When he took on the mantle of band leader following his father's death, Mercer Ellington insisted that musicians in The Duke Ellington Orchestra, played solos precisely as they were heard on the original records:[11]

> When we play Pop's tunes, we do them verbatim. I want the sound of everything that was there, including the solos, because I don't think that anyone today can concoct a solo that fits this music better than what Tricky Sam Nanton or Lawrence Brown or Cootie Williams played on it. I want to hear those same notes. (Popa: 2004)

Not all of the ghost bands relied on note perfect copying, some made use of personal interpretation to take the music forward in the style of its creator. Critical opinion on this level of deviation from the original text still remains divided – there are leaders who are determined to stamp out the practice – while others argue in favour of allowing the continuation of the repertoire under new direction. Gary Giddens, jazz critic and artistic director of the American Jazz Orchestra argues on behalf of the latter category:

> I think the parallel you would want to make is that of a great symphony orchestra. Just because Bernstein leaves or Boulez leaves doesn't mean that you sink the New York Philharmonic; you just hire another conductor. With a really distinguished ensemble you can do that. (Giddens, quoted in Friedman 2008)

Cover Bands: Transatlantic Supply and Demand

If the ghost bands are a distant cousin of the modern tribute bands, the pop and soul cover groups of the 1960s are a much closer relation. Their appearance at this particular juncture was due to a combination of audience demand and technological innovation. Although radio and records were popular music's initial channel of communication, this broadcasting hegemony was overturned by the introduction of new musical instruments and equipment. Acoustic instruments in the early days, had been unwieldy and difficult to hear in a packed club but electric guitars could be amplified, allowing musicians working in small groups to be heard. Eventually, the rock combo superseded the big bands thereby establishing a new format for the delivery of popular music. With the help of modern technology, cover bands were able to offer fans live versions of the popular songs currently dominating the charts and airwaves. Eventually, growing demand for live entertainment led to a proliferation of such bands touring both the UK and the US until, even the smallest of towns could support a few clubs offering live band nights.

There is confusion over the use of the terms "cover" and "tribute," however, although they are used interchangeably, the former predates the latter and was in common terminology during the 1960s. Jourard (1998: 60) describing the distinction, explains that, whereas cover bands will usually perform the work of a variety of artists (sometimes incorporating this with music they have written themselves), most tribute acts specialize in the faithful reproduction of the repertoire of a specific artist or band and do not as a rule, attempt to perform their own work. Within a live set a cover band will typically adopt an eclectic temporal approach, moving seamlessly backwards and forwards from one decade to another, offering a snapshot of a broad range of popular songs associated with various artists. In terms of entertainment potential, the heterogeneity of the cover band repertoire, lends itself to a much broader audience than that of the more specialized tribute, one of the main reasons why this type of entertainment continues to flourish.

Playing covers provides musicians with a steady income but those who choose this route are liable to be judged as lacking in ambition or creative acumen. This suggest that a strict line is drawn between musicians who play covers and those who write their own music, however, as Shuker (2008: 130) points out, performing covers is essential to the rock and pop apprenticeship. Since many internationally acclaimed artists played covers at the start of their careers, his observations are borne out by recordings drawn from The Beatles' and The Rolling Stones' early output. In 1964 The Rolling Stones produced cover versions of Chuck Berry's *Carol*, Norman Petty and Charles Hardin's *Not Fade Away* and Leiber and Stoller's *Poison Ivy* (indeed, their eponymous debut album featured only one self-written song). In fact, the Stones even released a version of The Beatles' *I Wanna Be Your Man* in 1962, while The Beatles included covers within their early repertoire, notably Chuck Berry's *Roll Over Beethoven* in 1963 and the Meredith Wilson ballad, *Till There Was You* in 1964.

In the UK, the early cover bands offered audiences live versions of the most up-to-date chart music and their popularity with fans at the time, indicates that they were happy to pay to hear these renditions of contemporary hit records. Although by this time most young people could afford to buy records, the cover bands offered the thrill of live music and the all-important social experience of dancing, in a period when the concept of the discotheque was still in its infancy. American soul music, was a particularly popular feature of the bands' repertoire: as a dance genre, it was enjoyed by both sexes and at this time, indigenous soul was thin on the ground. As Borthwick and Moy (2004: 7) explain, despite producing successful soul artists, such as Dusty Springfield, Cliff Bennett and Chris Farlowe, the UK lacked the songwriting and production teams central to the success of the American version. Cover bands in Britain were also able to capitalize on the fact that American soul artists rarely toured the UK. Indicative of the high status of dance based cover bands, Geno Washington and the Ram Jam Band achieved mainstream chart success with two albums of live versions of American soul music.[12]

The Impact of British Music on the American Cover Scene

Across the Atlantic, where British music was much in demand, the UK cover scene was played out in reverse. In the US, the 1960s was characterized by intense and rapid social change, where music played a pivotal role in the lives of young people, both in articulating the values of youth, and creating new ways of socializing and experiencing music. The changing cultural climate is described by a local musician who played in a cover band at the time:

> You've got to remember that the 60s was a new horizon. The values that Conservative America had grown up with since the wars (2 and Korea) were about to disappear. Music was the vehicle. Television was everywhere, and radio was going crazy. My parents didn't have American Bandstand or AM rock radio. I was 18 in 1964, it was incredible. I couldn't take in all the new stuff that was happening fast enough. Girls not only became sexually liberated, but they could go to the clubs (which catered only to teens) and not only be entertained, but get as close to whatever their fantasy was at that time. It may have been music, dress, hair styles, boys playing music exactly as they heard it on the radio. It had to be a turn on. (Mark Martinko, email, May 2007)

The impact on the live music scene was felt immediately:

> In Phoenix, a bunch of nightclubs sprang up in a matter of one year. The choices of what music a band wanted to play was really dictated by what the people wanted to hear, and what was being played on the radio. All you had to do was listen to the radio or buy the record, learn the songs and when you got 40 to 60 songs, you did an audition. Clubs were screaming for bands. (Mark Martinko, email, May 2007)

The fact that British bands made infrequent visits to the US only served to heighten enthusiasm for cover acts capable of offering UK pop in their repertoire and demand was further accelerated by the 'British Invasion' following the arrival of The Beatles in New York. As British music rose in the US charts, live cover bands were able to fulfil the unrequited desires of an audience anxious to experience something resembling the real thing. In a book chronicling the live music scene in Arizona, local music historian Ed Wincentsen (2002: 12) describes his excitement, on discovering two such bands: the Spiders (whose lead singer reminded him of Mick Jagger) and The Vibratos, who were billed as "the closest thing as The Beatles to ever hit the valley."

British music lovers were invited to come along – not just to hear the music but to behave like Beatles' fans too. This is clearly signified in a contemporary poster where those who come to see The Vibratos are invited to: "Scream along with the Blonde Beatle" and, for those who preferred the tougher image of rival band The Rolling Stones, Wincentsen remembered a Phoenix band billed as The American Rolling Stones:

> They played ALL Stones music. I guess you could say that they were the first tribute band. They kind of dressed like the Stones, but some

> of them had long hair and others just had regular hairstyles. They even had guitars like the Stones. They played at Christown Mall on the weekends, after the mall had closed and they opened up the foyer for the band and the dancers. (Ed Wincentsen, interview, May 2007)

Demonstrating the difficulty in separating popular music from contemporary fashion, the burgeoning troop of cover bands began to adopt the appropriate look in order to bring authenticity to their take on the British style. This was an important marketing tool in a crowded market, where the right image could secure a higher fee. In words of one musician, the "identikit" approach to Britishness required a rather exotic combination of clothing and instrumentation for a nation brought up on rockabilly and rock'n'roll.

> Just about all the bands (when they were doing cover songs) tried to sound exactly like the group that did the song. I was guilty in trying to get the look of Peter and Gordon, as I wore glasses and the (almost Buddy Holly look) made it easier to wear them on stage. We had a group called Phil and the Frantics, that tried to sing and play and look exactly like the Dave Clark Five. I believe that everybody tried to look and sound and play exactly like the person that did the song originally. That's what brought in the money. Many of the bands starting in 63 and 64, imitated The Beatles/Gerry and the Pacemakers look. No collar, no lapel jackets, thin ties, straight leg pants, Beatle Boots. Our band did the same ... [and] if you remember, hardly any bands used keyboards, except blues bands. When the Animals, Gerry and the Pacemakers, Zombies and Kinks came along, everybody had to have a Vox Keyboard. I think the English grabbed the US sound later and the US grabbed the look and style the UK presented. (Trikker, email, May 2007)

The cover bands on both side of the Atlantic clearly fulfilled similar roles in relocating music and offering the excitement of the live music experience via a set packed with chart favourites, but their audience was restricted to the younger end of the age spectrum whereas nowadays, the appeal of cover bands is much broader. They are no longer affiliated with youth or fashionable subcultures, functioning instead as a mainstay of popular entertainment and demonstrating that many are still happy to pay to enjoy live pop music in a local context, regardless of whether it is played by the "original" musicians.

The Impact of Discotheques on the Live Music Scene

The expansion of the live music scene in the 1960s was made possible because of the arrival of cheaper, portable equipment, but the impact of new technology on the live sector has not always been entirely positive. It appears to have had a negative impact on employment, a trend noted by both Frith (1987) and Sanjek and Sanjek (1991), who found a decline in job opportunities for live musicians as the medium became more home-centred. Employment for those playing in cover bands was further diminished by the emergence of a disco scene in the 1970s. According to Haslam (2000) discotheques originated in Paris during the Second World War when the Nazis banned jazz and fans subsequently took to the cellars to enjoy recorded versions of their favourite music. By the early 1960s most major international cities had followed the trend, making discos an accepted aspect of urban nightlife, but this had a knock-on effect on the popularity of live music as Haslam explains:

> Although live bands still played in clubs, pre-recorded music played by DJs had become an accepted part of a night out. In the Fifties an infrastructure of record hops, platter parties and juke-box joints had developed in America, and Jamaican sound systems had served Britain's black communities with Nat King Cole, calypso and early forms of reggae. In Britain, by 1960 La Discothèque had opened in Wardour Street, and clubs such as the Place in Hanley and the Plaza in Manchester had instituted disc-only sessions. (Haslam 2000)

The consequences for those committed to playing live covers was particularly severe, as Adrian Gregory, a musician with over 40 years' experience of the covers scene recalls:

> In the sixties, you were either an original band playing your own music with ambitions of fame and fortune, or a jobbing band, playing the hits of the day to supplement your day job earnings. Discos emerged in the seventies and rose to dominate the market for general pop music performance. Virtually overnight, nightclubs and village hall hops were taken over by discos and cover bands went into decline. Original bands doing their "own thing" have always found their own market in universities and specialist talent breaking venues and were unaffected by the rise of disco. (Adrian Gregory, interview, August 2005)

They may have fallen out of favour at the height of disco mania and the rise and fall of cover groups demonstrates the sensitive nature of the live music sector to wider developments across the industry.[13] Nevertheless, cover acts, are a remarkably durable entertainment model and, despite facing competition from the specialist tributes and pop impersonators, they continue to fulfil a role in popular entertainment, while providing employment for local musicians. In the words of one "weekend warrior":

> From the lows of the eighties, demand for live music at "middle of the road venues" and general functions such as weddings, bar mitzvahs and birthdays, has visibly risen, particularly in recent years. That demand has been supplied by the body of pragmatic musicians who want to play live but do not expect to make a living from their original work. (Adrian Gregory, interview, August 2005)

Pop Impersonators and Parody Bands

The primary purpose of the music revivals discussed thus far, has been with conservation or representation of the music and not necessarily the personal identity of the original artist. Musicians working in cover and ghost bands were not pop impersonators, as the concept had yet to be fully developed, but subsequent initiatives in the field of popular entertainment began to draw more on the personality and physical appearance of the archetype. For the source of pop music's "parodic turn," fingers normally point to the culture of impersonation centred around Elvis Presley, both prior to his untimely demise in 1977, and thereafter in significantly increasing numbers and subtypes.[14]

In addition to his role in widening semiotic participation, Elvis must be one of the few stars whose afterlife as a signifier commenced long before his death. It could even be argued that he initiated his own posthumous career path in the film *Love Me Tender* (1956) where, following a tragic love triangle, Elvis's character is shot dead only to reappear as a ghostly apparition at his own funeral. The decision to superimpose Presley's image in the sky was simply designed to pacify distraught fans but the consequences were far reaching in establishing both the Elvis cult and the model for a pop or rock afterlife. One of the first artists to capitalize on Elvis's identity did so during his lifetime: the R&B singer Jackie Wilson was the first to be credited with undertaking an element of impersonation. By introducing Presley impressions into his stage show during the 1950s, he unwittingly opened the floodgates. American performance artists and entertainer Andy Kaufman is another cited amongst the first to mimic Elvis. Described as a "radical" comic (Connor 2004: 108) Kaufman performed a number of alter-egos and seems to have been more concerned with interrogating the American Dream than with Elvis Presley's music per se and in this sense, his work cannot be conceived as a serious musical tribute.

Like Elvis, The Beatles attracted comic homage relatively early in their career and there are several lighthearted records dedicated to them. In 1964, *We Love You Beatles* by The Carefrees and *A Letter to The Beatles* by male quartet, The Four Preps, both surfaced on the Billboard chart and in the same year the singles, *My Boyfriend Got A Beatle Haircut*, by Donna Lynn and *The Boy With The Beatle Hair*, by The Swans achieved chart success. These pop songs were filled with humorous references to the Fab Four but they hardly represented a serious attempt to cannibalize their identity. Taking a step further in the direction of impersonation, the parodic British pop bands of the 1960s and 1970s, also relied on humour to diffuse their efforts. The Barron Knights were one of the first to navigate a career as pop impersonators, beginning their career as a straight vocal harmony group, working as a support act to both The Beatles and The Rolling Stones during the 1960s and after several years in this role, moved into comedy and parodying the work of contemporary artists. Their instantly recognizable and amusing impersonations achieved chart success in 1964 with the single *Call Up The Groups*: a parodic medley, which somehow overcame copyright restrictions. The recording featured the group simulating the sounds of The Beatles, The Dave Clark Five, The Bachelors and The Searchers in a comic scenario where the famous bands were called up to join the British Army.[15]

By bringing comedy to the musical and vocal impersonation of various artists, The Barron Knights operated rather like a hybrid comic cover band whereas, by parodying the identity and music of a single group, the work of The Rutles, took parody a step further towards the modern the tribute act. Essentially a fictional Beatles band, The Rutles, was created by Neil Innes and Eric Idle during the mid-1970s. Starting life in a comedy sketch on the BBC television series *Rutland Weekend Television*, the group achieved notoriety with the 1978 "mockumentary" film, *All You Need is Cash.* Subtitled, "The musical legend which will last a lunchtime," the film featured a pastiche of Beatles songs which were later released as a soundtrack on their eponymous debut album. In the film, the chronology of the Rutles' career, closely resembles that of The Beatles. The story begins with the formation of the band and their experiences in performing in Hamburg and Liverpool before moving on to the recording session of their first hit *Number One* (a parody of the 1963 hit, *Twist and Shout*). *All You Need is Cash* features parodies of *A Hard Day's Night* (1964) and *Help* (1965), which are presented as *A Hard Day's Rut* and *Ouch*, and their albums *Rubber Soul* (1965) and *Sergeant Pepper's Lonely Hearts Club Band* (1965) with *Rutle Soul* and *Sergeant Rutter's Only Darts Club Band.* Neil Innes, a former member of Bonzo Dog Doodah Band, created the soundtrack as well as 20 of the film's songs, each of which is a pastiche of a Beatles track. In fact, the content was so close to original Beatles' compositions, he faced a legal challenge from the owners of The Beatles' catalogue and was forced to swear that he had worked only from memory and had not attempted a deliberate copy. The British parody bands' heavy-handed use of comedy probably helped them to avoid some of the legal problems and charges of identity theft encountered by their followers.

The First Tribute Bands

Impetus for the first tribute acts did not stem from satiric impulses – particular factors which led to their appearance included a desire to enjoy rock at close range, nostalgia, and a growing demand for live performances of the work of deceased or otherwise unavailable artists. During the 1960s, prior to the advent of stadium rock, the majority of touring bands played clubs and theatres, however, successful groups inevitably outgrew the smaller venues, and larger stadiums offered increased earnings for bands such as The Stones, U2 and Led Zeppelin. Popular acts capable of attracting audiences of over 50,000, having quit the small club circuit, soon learnt how to make the large stage work for them.[16] Stadium rock called for a new aesthetic, defined by a greater emphasis on showmanship, high volume and catchy anthemic songs. Massive venues could accommodate the maximum number of fans but for many, the experience was and is, a disappointment. The high price of tickets and refreshments and the impersonal nature of the event led to lower levels of satisfaction. In particular, the distance between artists and audience creates a chasm, despite the employment of state-of-the art technology such as big screens. As Auslander explains, the technology employed to bridge the gap only serves to heighten the schism.

> the use of giant video screens at rock concerts provides a means of creating in a large-scale event the effect of "intimacy and immediacy" associated with smaller live events. In order to retain those characteristics, large-scale events must surrender a substantial measure of their liveness to mediatization. (Auslander quoted in Homan 2006: 37)

The appearance of tribute acts helped to draw fans back to the small, friendly local environments of small theatres and live music venues, environments which were struggling to attract pop and rock fans by the late 1970s. By this time, the cover acts which used to play there were no longer fashionable, and although audiences enjoy live music in an intimate setting, they are notoriously reluctant to pay to see unknown artists performing an unfamiliar repertoire. As an updated, more specialized form of cover act, tributes were able to offer the winning combination of novelty and familiarity, giving music lovers a tried and trusted repertoire. Although they drew on aspects of the templates provided by ghost, parody and cover bands, in simulating identity and making use of period instruments and clothing, they were distinctive enough from their predecessors to inspire curiosity.

The origins of the first tribute bands are obscure: Homan (2006: 6) cites British acts The Counterfeit Stones (1979), The Bootleg Beatles (1980) and Australian band, The Beatnix (1980) as key contenders. Other candidates include the American band, The Rolling Clones (1979) and the Beatles tribute Rain (mid-1970s). For these early groups, musical theatre offered an entertainment model ripe for adaptation, and the approach was adapted for the complex stage shows of The Bootleg Beatles, Bjorn Again and The Counterfeit Stones. Rather than relying solely on music, these acts began to incorporate multimedia and elements of comedy into their performance. Musical theatre also provided a corps of musicians with the appropriate skills required to launch these shows: indeed for some of them, the move into playing tribute was a logical progression from working in the realm of film or theatre. According to Homan (2006: 41) Chris O'Neill formed The Backbeat Beatles after playing the role of George Harrison in the Channel Four film *Backbeat* (1994), and Neil Harrison, prior to performing in The Bootleg Beatles was a former member of the cast of *Beatlemania.*

Reasons for the appearance of three of the earliest tribute bands, The Bootleg Beatles, Rain and The Beatnix, can be attributed to an emotional vacuum created by the original band's break up in 1970. In terms of its emotional impact, The Beatles' demise should not be underestimated – fans reeling from the shock of the split – continued to hanker for a reunion, but despite rumours, their wishes were not fulfilled and no outlet was available for the pent-up emotions. The process of grieving, is not restricted to death and the symptoms triggered by any major loss, can be very similar to those experienced by the bereaved. In study of death, dying and bereavement, Kubler Ross (1973) observed various important stages through which the bereaved must pass in order to deal with their grief. People tend alternate between states of denial, anger and depression before moving towards the final stage of acceptance and within the grief process their desire to be united with the lost loved one may lead them to experience and sometimes welcome hallucinations of the deceased. It is easy to see how, in the process of coming to terms with the loss of The Beatles, their tributes fulfilled an important role in representing a tangible link with lost love ones, allowing the grief feelings to be discharged.

According to Mark Lewis, founder member of one of the earliest Beatles' tributes Rain, the group was formed in the mid-1970s when he joined forces with four local musicians, to play live sets incorporating a substantial proportion of Beatles' covers. Rain's original ambition to secure a record deal was not realized and eventually, as the rising wave of nostalgia led to even greater demand for Beatles' numbers, they concentrated solely on this aspect of their work. In 1978 their career was further boosted by an invitation to record the soundtrack for the film *Birth of the Beatles*, a fictional recreation of the foursome's early life. Rain went on to hire four alumni of the stage show Beatlemania and are still performing The Beatles' repertoire over 30 years later. The show did not just inspire would-be Beatles' tributes, it also provided the inspiration for Jimmy Lee's Rolling Stones tribute, The Rolling Clones:

> I started The Rolling Clones after being entertained by many Elvis impersonators and then after seeing the Broadway show Beatlemania. I thought WOW how would a Rolling Stones tribute work out? The band was formed around 1978. It was rehearsed for about 4 months, performing small shows to test the reaction of the audience which truly took us by surprise! (Jimmy Lee, email, July 2007)

Despite having only rehearsed for a short time, the group quickly progressed to bigger and better things, "We really were not ready in my opinion when we started doing major large shows and then we were asked to appear in Las Vegas where we performed for two weeks ... doing three shows a night."

In the UK The Bootleg Beatles inspired the first British tribute to the Rolling Stones, an undertaking initiated by founder member Steve Elson. Elson had already formed a precursor known as The Strolling Boulders, in the unlikely location of Ndola in the Zambia, whilst acting as tour manager for pop group The Equals. When he returned to Britain he decided to reform the group under a different name in response to a creative project brief:

> I formed the Strolling Bones in 1982 to cut a record for a label owned by Baron Bentlink who wanted a rock record for the troops in the Falklands. He considered the Stones to be the essence of English rock'n'roll. I'd just seen The Bootleg Beatles the weekend before and thought that with the studio line up who'd just recorded, we'd make a cracking live band. And for three years we did. We must have played every university and college in Britain. It wasn't a costume act and there was little corporate or night club work then. Theatres were a definite "No No." (Steve Elson, interview, September 2007)

Clearly the band were satisfying a demand but the full potential of the tribute concept was yet to be developed.

Michael White and The White: the first Tribute band

According to Lewis (1991) The White,[17] performing the music of Led Zeppelin, were the first band to be billed as a "tribute," thereby creating the conceptual term for a new form of entertainment, something to be distinguished from the less fashionable cover groups or the tackier efforts of the pop impersonators. While homages to The Beatles could be seen as a providing a physical repository for fans' unreleased emotions, The White, like the first Rolling Stones' tributes, capitalized instead, on the extraordinary demand for live rock music. Zeppelin's power to draw an audience was such that, with each successive tour, they attracted an ever larger crowd. In 1973, they broke The Beatles' record audience at Shea Stadium by drawing 56,800 fans to Tampa Stadium, and in the years which followed, they continued to break all records. By 1977 they broke a world record, playing to over 76,000 fans at a concert in Michigan.[18] Zeppelin's international popularity was established mainly through their commitment to touring the US and in 1969, 33 out of 139 shows were performed there, however from 1971 they limited touring to alternate years only. This decision would have left many fans disappointed and, bearing this in mind, it is not surprising that Zeppelin fans were amongst the first to embrace the concept of live rock tribute.

Unlike some of their fellows, The White have gained critical acceptance within the official rock community. The heavy metal bible *Kerrang* (June 2002), refers to them as, "a remarkable American Led Zeppelin tribute band", and their live musical homage, covering the entire back catalogue of 74 songs, has been seen by 2.5 million people in the US and Canada. Frontman Michael White began his career with a band known as The Boyz. They were well-received in the Los Angeles area, gaining sufficient status to be placed as a headline act but regardless of their popularity, The Boyz remained unsigned leading them to split up in 1977, at which point, Michael formed The White. The plan was not to exploit Led Zeppelin's work intentionally, but Michael's vocal and physical resemblance to Robert Plant, led record label bosses to judge The White's work as too similar to Zeppelin's to warrant a signing.

Following a stint in the band London (which later became Mötley Crüe), he eventually returned to work full-time with The White, however, continued comparisons with Led Zeppelin drove the group to focus their energies solely on this aspect of their work. The change was a wise career move which resulted in a series of sell-out gigs across California and two decades of non-stop touring.

The response of the original Zeppelin was overwhelmingly positive – when Michael White finally met up with Robert Plant in 1983, he was introduced by him to a manager at Zeppelin's record label, Atlantic Records. The liaison produced a signing in 1985 and, after working with Zeppelin's producer on some demo discs, a recording contract followed. With further success, the band's audience grew, so much so, that during the 1980s numbers attending their shows outstripped those paying to see Aerosmith on the same night. An album entitled *Michael White* was released in 1987, only to be met by yet another wave of Led Zeppelin comparisons but critical reservations do not appear to have hindered their progress. The White have shared the stage with many high-profile artists including James Brown, Eric Clapton, Elton John and

Prince: they are also one of the few tribute acts to have achieved success with recordings of the works of their archetype.

Promoters were initially suspicious of the tribute concept and had to be educated because, according to Michael, some of them were under the impression that The White were going to show films or bootleg videos rather than perform live music. Robert Godwin, a club manager and promoter, reflects on his first encounter with the band in the early 1980s.

> It was my responsibility to book the bands into my club, the Orient Express, and to that end I dealt with several booking agencies. I had a deal with the biggest of the agencies that they would bring me the best acts but the smaller agencies were always knocking on my door trying to steal slots for their acts. (Robert Godwin, email, May 2009)

He received a press kit from a rival agency, featuring a photograph of what he assumed to be Led Zeppelin. On further inspection the band were described as "A Tribute to Led Zeppelin" but at the time, the concept was not understood and the club booked either original or cover acts:

> At this time I was bringing a different band in seven nights a week but they were usually either established names, cover bands or up and coming original acts. The roster included people like Joe Perry, Rick Derringer, Mountain, Steve Marriott, Steppenwolf mixed in with original local bands. On the weekends the cover bands would provide mostly mixed renderings of popular rock songs. I had only twice before been offered a band that only played songs by one artist. There was a Rolling Stones band called "The Blushing Brides" and a really good Hendrix band called "Fire." (Robert Godwin, email, May 2009)

Godwin acknowledged that he was taking a risk: "These were VERY early days for 'tribute' bands, as I said, we had only been offered two between September 1981 and October 1982, and as good as they both were, they were both just starting out." His decision to hire the band was mainly influenced by the high quality of their press kit (which contained photographs taken by a noted Zeppelin photographer) and The White's proven track record evidenced by their press clippings,[19] nevertheless, booking the group involved taking a calculated risk:

> The White had been playing something like 250 shows a year for at least two years by the time I heard of them, and some of those shows were in front of 5000 people in soft-seat theatres ... so I booked them without hearing them, for a Wednesday night.

Godwin, who admits to being, "one of the world's foremost Led Zeppelin collectors," was not disappointed:

> White's knowledge of Led Zeppelin's music is unparalleled in my experience. I may know things like, what song they played, where and when, but he knows exactly HOW they played it. What instruments, what studio effects, what key, and what were the tricks and overdubs. There is little doubt (in my mind at least), that Michael White and The White were clearly the first to take that theatrical Beatlemania concept and turn it into a viable touring band. (Robert Godwin email, May 2009)

The White, like the The Bootleg Beatles and Counterfeit Stones were pioneers and as such, could trade upon their novelty factor, but their success inspired other musicians and promoters to take advantage of the potential offered by the conceptual model. Homage acts were quickly embedded within the live entertainment industry, illustrating the flexibility of that sector as well as its ability to respond to extra-market demand. The model flourished as various subtypes emerged, each catering for different segments of the market and although the idea has yet to be adopted officially by the record industry, tributes complement and enhance the existing output of CDs, DVDS and rock and pop memorabilia.

4 Establishing a Typology

"Art begins in imitation and ends in innovation." Mason Cooley

Adorno, arguing that popular music only offered pseudo-individualism thereby making it incapable of delivering any true variety, said that: "The whole structure of popular music is standardized, even where the attempt is made to circumvent standardization. Standardization extends from the most general features to the most specific ones" (Adorno quoted in Shuker 2001: 19). Uniformity may well be one of the less desirable effects of mass-production but when it comes to the sphere of consumption, the situation is rather different. The number of texts in circulation is limited and bound by corporate objectives, but when it comes to the interpretation of these texts, cultural populists (Willis 1990; Fiske 1989a,b) point to the seemingly endless opportunities they provide for polysemic amusement.

In the live music sector, much of the standardization informing the record industry may be relinquished, partly because it is more difficult to enforce or police in the less structured environment of pubs, independent clubs and small theatres, but also because there is a demand for deviations from the standard text. Indeed diversity is positively celebrated in the parallel universe inhabited by tributes and impersonators, as the line up at a recent Beatles' festival reveals. The event, which permitted a baffling array of bands to offer their own unique take on the work of the Fab Four, included the following acts:

> Japanese Beatles, Norwegian Beatles, German Beatles (two groups actually). Swedish Beatles, Canadian Beatles. American Beatles. Scottish Beatles. American Beatles pretending to be English. Costumed Beatles. Uncostumed Beatles. Submoronic Beatles (The Yellow SubMorons, tribute band for the Rutles, the fictitious parody group of The Beatles). Blue Beatles. Accoustic Beatles. And we can't forget two different Wings – one from England. And Instant Karma, the John Lennon tribute band.[1]

A study of entertainment agency websites reveals an equally mixed bag. Alongside those dedicated to Elvis, Abba and The Beatles, there are a always a few homages to more obscure artists, making one wonder at the sheer range of opportunities for mimesis. What is more, far from being uniform in character, the aims and scope of the acts available for hire differs considerably. There is something of a dichotomy for example, between those musicians who concentrate solely on the work of individual artists, and the generalist entertainers whose brief requires them to offer far broader coverage of particular music genres. Entertainment agencies don't just stick to musical mimicry either, they have been quick to exploit the growing obsession with celebrity identity – hence the appearance of individuals performing characters from successful films and celebrity look-alikes, who make a living out of portraying those who inhabit the Hollywood "A" list. Operating as live, floating signifiers, they illustrate how in the twenty-first century, mobilized and distributed way beyond the original context of production, stardom is no longer subject to the absolute authority of corporate control, as exclusivity and individuality are sacrificed to feed a growing appetite for bargain-basement fame.

This chapter explores the multifariousness of the scene, showing how by constantly rehashing the work of existing artists, it might appear to uphold the rather limited conservative ideologies and ambitions of the music industry. I will reveal how imitative entertainment is also capable of much more than this in that rather than affirming corporate ideologies, it is sometimes used to resist and subvert industry stereotypes, ideologies and norms. In this sense, the subversive potential of live tributes illustrates Middleton's (2001: 11) point that, "the best commentary on music comes in the form of the music itself." With this in mind, I will be looking at examples of individual musicians and artists to allow them to speak for themselves before looking finally, at what might be referred to as "extreme tributes." These are the esoteric acts which inhabit a musical "third space" where hegemonic practices are not only challenged but abandoned altogether, in favour of a form of entertainment which hovers in a no-man's land, somewhere between the tasteless and the bizarre.

A Darwinian Struggle

Who is being imitated and why? When it comes to proportional representation, it does seem that certain artists get more than their fair share of imitators, with the vast majority paying homage to a pretty limited number of acts and genres. Rock and pop are without doubt more popular than other genres, but this hegemony can be explained by Borthwick and Moy's (2004) supposition that the inherent elasticity of the metagenres of rock and pop allows them to "transcend historical epochs." Less easily mobilized genres such as progressive rock and Britpop are, they claim, "intrinsically tied to an era, a mode of production [or] a Zeitgeist" (2004: 3). Their observations are certainly borne out in a UK tribute top ten where almost all of the acts listed, fit neatly into the categories of either rock or mainstream pop.

Most Tributed Artists in the UK in 2004 (MCPS-PRS Alliance)

(1) Elvis Presley
(3) Abba
(7) Robbie Williams
(-) Neil Diamond
(4) Queen/Freddie Mercury
(-) Frank Sinatra
(2) The Beatles
(-) Meatloaf
(-) Rod Stewart
(6) The Blues Brothers

Source: *The Independent on Sunday*, 28 March 2004.

Clearly, the excessive number of rock and pop acts can be accounted for but notwithstanding the hegemony of rock and pop, even a cursory study of the average entertainment agency website, indicates that Abba, Queen and Beatles tributes are legion, whereas other well-known artists appear to have vanished without a simulacrum in sight.[2] These findings will no doubt reinforce the popular view of the tribute as shamelessly populist but alongside the everyday fodder, there are some decidedly esoteric and unlikely subtypes out there. Lurking in the shadows of the mainstream, these acts operate along the lines of a counterculture, offering more than just a variation on a common theme, they demonstrate high levels of imagination, humour and a determination to shock. Unlike the more earnest or respectful homages to the dead and defunct, they mobilize détournement as a means of critiquing or subverting the intentions of their archetype, thereby challenging many of the meanings assigned to the original texts. Unfettered by some of the constraints imposed on the original artists, these "alternative" acts have more freedom to challenge boundaries. Emancipated from the need to follow the rules, some are decidedly eccentric while others in the true spirit of rock and roll, are determined to flout everything from standards of good taste to decency laws.

There is for example the group Mandonna, an all male dance troupe fronted by a bearded "Madonna" who, with the help of a live band, pays outrageously high camp homage to the Material Girl. Then there is Tragedy, a New York based, heavy metal band who honour the schmaltzy disco harmonies of The Bee Gees with a crescendo of angry, crashing chords. Surely though, the "mother" of all tributes must be the exhibitionist, leather-clad rockers, Nudist

Priest, a band which enacts naked homage to heavy metal icons Judas Priest. Lastly, if you have every wondered what hip-hop icons Cypress Hill might sound like if their music was performed in big-band style, you need look no further than Richard Cheese and his band, Lounge Against The Machine![3]

Before embarking on a more detailed study of the different types, a reflection on the Darwinian character of the world of ersatz entertainment seems an appropriate context for deeper investigation. There is clearly an element of natural selection going on: although it is already established that rock and pop stars have a greater than average chance of attracting imitators than do practitioners of other genres, there are still questions to be answered. Why have certain artists fallen by the wayside, failing to attract many, or in some cases any imitators, when others have such a surfeit? Clearly some artists are more memorable than others but since the act of remembering is itself so complex, it is not easy to establish precisely what features will guarantee a place in the popular memory. Memory is both an individual, private experience as well as a collective one which forms an essential aspect of our personal and group identities. Without a past we lack a meaningful present, but the act of remembering, whether in an individual or collective sense, is a process which can never be complete and in terms of significance, what is forgotten can be just as compelling as what is remembered. Shared memory is of particular interest precisely because it transcends the limitations of the individual psyche. Where personal memories are restricted by an individual's capacity to prioritize and maintain facts images and narratives, collective memory is formed and determined by groups, a process which implies contestation, negotiation and sharing.

Pondering on the mysteries of collective musical memory Frith (1996: 3) asks, "Who would have thought that 1990s nostalgia for glam rock would focus not on Marc Bolan or Slade or Sweet but on Gary Glitter?" Who indeed, but we might also ask why Cliff Richard, the UK's homegrown Prince of Rock and Roll and icon of the film musical, has such paltry handful of followers while Elvis and Robbie Williams have so many? Reasons are both elusive and inconsistent. In a study of the phenomenology of memory, Ricoeur (2004: 66) refers to, "the weakness inherent in both the preservation of [memory] traces and their evocation" – what will be remembered in the collective musical consciousness is just as difficult to predict as what will be forgotten. Straw (2000: 175) suggests that our attempts to understand the mysteries of musical memory are hindered by our tendency to tidy up the past – making it fit neatly into categories – with styles and artists following one from another in an orderly fashion. Moreover, he argues "because of its perceived immateriality, popular music has been studied in ways which emphasize change over time, which are fixated on the succession and seriality of musical texts and styles." He goes on to remind us that the past is much messier than we would like it to be, and, rather than following a logical path, cultural texts have a tendency to accumulate in a less predictable manner.

Memory certainly requires a strong element of forgetfulness. We simply cannot remember everything – for various reasons we may choose to forget once cherished memories and associated artefacts. The tangible evidence of the music rejected by popular consent in charity shop odd bins, invites us to ponder on the fidelity of music consumers: a meaningful cultural text from one era may lack resonance for subsequent audiences and is thus rejected or in other circumstances, it may provoke an entirely different response to that originally intended.

> As cultural artefacts become dated, one effect of this dating is that differences in prestige and ambition dissolve within the shared markers of a period sensibility. Aesthetic judgments about different degrees of seriousness or achievement will come to seem less pertinent than the anthropological noting of shifting collective perceptions and values. (Straw 2000: 175)

Like the recordings cast aside by the public the image and identity of artists can also become dated, making them less desirable, disposable even, and for these reasons – less in demand on the tribute scene.

Measuring Popularity

Are any factors more likely to ensure a place in the collective memory? Surely the most well-loved artists should attract more tributes? This ought be so if popularity was a reliable barometer of homage-worthiness but we need to be careful for there are shortcomings in applying crude quantitative methodologies as a research tool. Clearly something cannot by definition, be popular unless a lot of people like it but Storey (2001: 6) reminds us that: "on its own, a quantitative index is not enough to provide an adequate definition of popular culture." The value invested in popular music, is clearly too ambiguous and mutable to be determined by such measures on their own. Number crunching methods will not offer explanations as to *why* certain music has popular appeal and anyway, as shifts in taste and desire can so easily deflate the value of a once favoured commodity, their application is limited.

This certainly seems to be the case if we return to the example of Cliff Richard. There is no doubt that he was and is popular: an entry in *The Guinness Book of British Hit Singles* (2000: 355) names Cliff unequivocally as, "Britain's most successful solo vocalist."[4] He is credited with a staggering 64 UK

Top Ten entries and worldwide sales of over eighty-five million. Regardless of his unqualified popularity, entertainment agency Tributes Abroad (www.tributesabroad.co.uk/), offers a meagre three tributes to him, compared to Elton John's nine and Elvis Presley's 16 moreover, other UK agencies exhibit an equally inexplicable dearth of Cliffs.[5] Richard's record sales may be a mere drop in the musical ocean compared to Presley's estimated billion plus but his popularity is still significant. Nevertheless, his value as a signifier of social desire does not match his canonic status as an artist, suggesting that he has been sidelined for reasons other than measurable chart success.

The Benefits of an Untimely Departure

Cliff's problem may be attributed to the fact that he has simply lived too long! As the motto "Live Fast Die Young" permeates popular music, an untimely departure may add extra homage points. It would have been difficult for anyone to match Elvis's stature as a cultural icon when he was alive, and his posthumous success is equally peerless. Within the music industry, there are constant reminders that premature death is something of an occupational hazard – rock stars are almost twice as likely to die young as are members of the general public.[6] However in terms of raising popularity, rather than being a barrier to continuing success, death can open up further opportunities for commodification, bringing to mind DeLillo's reflections on the nature of modern death which, "has a life independent of us," moreover, "It is growing in prestige and dimension. It has a sweep it never had before. It continues to grow, to acquire breadth and scope, new outlets, new passages and means" (DeLillo 1985, quoted in Rodman 1996: 1).

Taking this into account, it is very tempting to relate Elvis's multitude of impersonators to his untimely departure, but death offers no fixed guarantee of retro-rock afterlife. In his heyday the British rock and roll singer Billy Fury achieved more UK chart hits during the 1960s than The Beatles (Rice and Roberts 2000: 203). Despite Fury's proven success and the fact that he died in 1983, he has only managed to attract a decidedly modest retinue of imitators. One of the largest UK entertainment agencies, Dansatak, offers just one tribute to Fury and further research reveals only a handful of others.[7] In common with his contemporary Cliff Richard, Fury's tributes do not match his success as a recording artist and yet, unlike Elvis, his premature departure failed to elevate his standing in the world of posthumous performance.

Then again, if we search for an example beyond the quirky parameters of British taste it is equally difficult to apply either the popularity paradigm or posthumous value added points to internationally famous pop duo, The Carpenters. The Grammy award winners were one of the most successful middle-of-the road acts of the 1970s. Their 1973 compilation album, *The Singles 1969–1973*, stayed in the US album charts for 115 weeks and *Rolling Stone* magazine voted the album *Close to You* (1970) one of the 500 greatest albums of all time (Levy 2003). Notwithstanding their staggering success and Karen Carpenter's tragic death at the age of 32, the duo's significance is not marked quantitatively by a cult tribute following.

Making Good Looks Count

If premature death and record sales are unpredictable indices of popularity – a distinctive look appears to provide a better than average chance of securing followers. Grossberg (1994: 54) was one of the first to note popular music's post-1960s shift away from sound suggesting that, "The visual (whether MTV, or youth films or even network television) is increasingly displacing sound as the locus of generational identification, differentiation, investment and occasionally even authenticity." A common characteristic shared by the most heavily impersonated artists, is a striking and instantly recognizable visual identity. The importance played by fashion and the visual in the construction of star identity, is acknowledged by a number of writers: from the general studies undertaken by Jones (1987), Sims (1999) and Gorman (2001) to the more specific (Mundy 2003; Bracewell 2008). Although fashionable in the broadest sense, it may be that The Carpenters and Cliff Richard lacked a sufficiently distinctive visual identity to attract an ersatz afterlife.

In Elvis Presley's case, image was fundamental to his success from the outset and Mundy (1999: 113) illustrates the extent to which it subsumed his vocal ability. He suggests that the airplay Elvis received was initially linked to reception of his live performances, arguing that, "It was the way he looked, just as much as how he sounded, that demanded attention and which created a sensation." Furthermore, he points to adverts for the artist's shows, where fans are invited to, "See" the artist singing *That's All Right* and *Blue Moon of Kentucky.* The following extracts from a contemporary review of one of his shows, indicate the extent to which Presley's vocal abilities were overshadowed by his image and performance style. Dick Williams of *The Daily Mirror* begins the review with a reference to Presley's glamorous stage outfit:

> Pandemonium took over from the time he swaggered triumphantly on stage like some ancient Caesar, resplendent in gold lame tux jacket with rhinestone lapels, until he weaved off at the end of his stint. It was almost impossible to hear the music despite a turned-up public address system. (Williams 1957)

By the end of the review there is still no mention of his vocal ability:

> The madness reached its peak at the finish with *Hound Dog*. Elvis writhed in complete abandon, hair hanging down over his face. He got down on the floor with a huge replica of the RCA singing dog and made love to it as if it were a girl. Slowly, he rolled over and over on the floor. (Williams 1957)

The distinctiveness and familiarity of Elvis's look makes it easy to replicate – a white jump suit, sunglasses, long black sideburns and a quiff – are all that is needed to connote "Elvisness."

In a similar manner, ABBA's ability to attract multiple imitators can be linked to their striking image. Surprisingly, in view of their vast legion of tributes, contemporary opinion on the foursome's live performance was somewhat lukewarm and despite a successful sell-out tour in 1977, they were criticized for a lack-lustre stage presence with one reviewer labelling the show "boring."[8] Their live performances may not have enjoyed critical acclaim but in terms of visual impact, the band more than compensated by making particularly effective use of video, a strategy which attracted worldwide interest in their camp fashion sensibility.[9] The ABBA videos also provide a valuable legacy for aspiring tribute artists, most of whom appear to have made use of them in determining wardrobe and performance style. Interestingly, although the videos offer a wealth of information on the band's wardrobe, like Elvis impersonator's, ABBA look-alikes invariably resort to a restricted number of signifiers. A survey of the promotional images of the entertainment agency Dansatak's (http://www.dansatak.com) 28 tributes to the band, indicates that for 90 per cent, essence of ABBA is connoted via the wearing of a signature style, white, satin karate suits, with a coloured trim. When compared with ABBA and Elvis, The Carpenters lack sufficient visual distinctiveness and their look cannot be distilled through means of semiotic shorthand, into an instantly recognizable image. The same could be said of Cliff Richard, whose early rebel image was eventually subsumed by a bland and wholesome identity, one which dismally fails to ignite the popular memory cells.

Approaches to the Creative Challenge

Regardless of the visual distinctiveness of the original artist, those charged with paying homage are divided as to how to go about the task in the first place. The main division is between ensembles committed to the faithful reproduction of visual identity and those which concentrate all their attentions on sound. It is also possible to distinguish between acts adhering religiously to the original repertoire and those introducing elements of improvisation and interpretation. Finally there is a hotchpotch of difficult-to-categorize bands offering a mixture of comedy, novelty, subversion and miscellaneous mayhem.[10] Disregarding the fact that they are accused of copying, it is interesting to note that no two tributes to an artist are quite alike even though they share the common goal of recreating an identity and repertoire. In attempting to do this, each faces a unique challenge because, through the art of performance, music taken from its quintessential context becomes something quite different and therefore, despite the fact that each aims to recreate the work of Led Zeppelin, the experience of a Lez Zeppelin gig is not the same as hearing and seeing Whole Lotta Led, Led Zepagain or Letz Zep. Each band offers the audience a unique blend of variables reflective of their age, gender, ability, equipment and personal approach to interpretation.

Musicians must decide whether to infuse an element of their own personality into the performance or try instead, to mimic the artist's identity faithfully. This is a question which perplexes performers and critics alike. Some musicians favour an approach resembling the classical style of acting, where thoughts and emotions are simulated through the use of external means such as vocal intonation or facial expression. The Bootleg Beatles for example, put all their energy into studious imitation, essentially acting in character and in doing so, minimizing the impact of their own personalities. Other performers are determined to stamp their own personality onto the work of the architect. Wayne Ellis of Limehouse Lizzy is clear regarding the parameters of his interpretation. He told me he was keen to remain congruent to his own performance style and personality, thus he made a conscious decision not to imitate Phil Lynott's stage presence (Figure 4.1). Nevertheless, despite avoiding outright impersonation, he does have the ability to communicate the essence of Phil Lynott's persona by drawing on his own inner resources. In this respect Ellis's approach mirrors that of the, "Method" school of acting where actors are encouraged to "live the part" while maintaining some degree of detachment to the character they are playing (Krasner 2000). By bringing truthful behaviour to imaginary circumstance, the method actor's main responsibility on stage is to be believable: this is achieved through the study and experience of subjective feelings an actor brings their part which, if successful, results in a very natural and believable style of performance.

Image versus Sound – The Look-Alikes

Regardless of which acting style (if any) is brought to the portrayal of the original, audiences generally prefer acts which invest in visual impersonation. The growth of look-alike entertainment is a reflection of a much more widespread inflation of the value of images in contemporary culture where,

Figure 4.1 Wayne Ellis (photograph Wayne Ellis, by permission)

according to Mirzoeff (1998: 3), "human experience is now more visual and visualised than ever before." With their carefully studied attempts to mimic identity, instruments, clothing and other ephemera, look-alike tributes clearly embody this argument. For the majority of acts there are limits – aesthetic as well as economic – and bands generally operate an element of temporal reductivism in their visual impersonation. This is particularly the case when bringing to life the identity of iconic acts with substantial repertoires. For example most Beatles' tributes offer a detailed portrayal of the band as they appeared in the early 1960s, making Pierre Cardin suits and mop top hairstyles de rigueur, whereas Elvis look-alikes appear to have settled en masse, for the King's appearance during the Las Vegas years so that it is rare to see the performer portrayed in the early stages of his career. Through repeated exposure to a limited set of visual signifiers, we eventually begin to associate them with the very essence of the original. This reductionism perfectly embodies Baudrillard's (1983) reflections on the signifier's omnipresence in postmodern culture and what he refers to as "the precession of the simulacra," where copies have taken on a life of their own. For Baudrillard images now pre-empt their source and, "It is no longer a question of imitation, nor duplication, nor even parody. It is a question of substituting the signs of the real for the real." So much so, that any Queen tribute presenting their Freddie Mercury kitted out in anything other than trademark yellow jacket or white tracksuit replete with regulation red stripes, runs the risk of being deemed "inauthentic" in the audience's eyes. Look-alikes may provide anything from a nodding resemblance to an eerie facsimile depending on factors such as physical and financial limitations as well as aesthetic or personal reasons. Physical limitations are particularly difficult to overcome: whilst wigs and make up can be used to great effect; age, gender, race and size present certain obstacles to credible representation. According to Paul Crook of the Sex Pistols Experience, their current Johnny Rotter was a replacement for an earlier frontman who gained too much weight and no longer looked sufficiently youthful to play the role convincingly (Figure 4.2).

Figure 4.2 The Sex Pistols Experience (photograph Kevin Ryan, by permission)

Five Star Homage – The Full Tributes

The problems of recruiting believable performers are multiplied several times over for the five star look-alikes, an elite group of ultimate doppelgangers referred to in the business as "full tributes". Due to the scale of their operation, full tributes are usually found in theatres and arenas rather than small music clubs and pubs, where they are able to offer an elaborate stage show. In addition to music, this may include comedy, drama and dance, film screenings, pyrotechnics or the use of props and special effects. They take imitation to the "nth" degree by providing the audience with an accurate copy of pretty much everything – from looks, accents and mannerisms – to period instrumentation and clothing. For lots of reasons this is a tall order, but those who take the most trouble will command the highest fees as Lenny Mann, author of the website Tribute City and member of Led Zepplica explains:

> If you look at the most successful tribute acts here is the States, they are the ones who emulate the whole package such as sound, appearance, onstage mannerisms, etc. My band Led Zepplica was selected by one of the biggest producers in North America to headline tours in Canada and USA playing the same venues as international recording acts. We have performed in front of thousands – emulating a live mid 70s Led Zeppelin concert. (Lenny Mann, email, January 2008)

No detail is too small or complex – complete set lists are slavishly copied, the characters and names of the original artists are parodied and in some cases – entire historical pop moments are meticulously re-enacted. In 2004, US Beatles' tribute Rain, relived The Beatles' 1964 arrival in America by staging a facimile event at the Seattle Museum of Flight. The spectacle, which took place 40 years to the minute when the Fab Four first arrived in New York, drew a crowd of over 7,000 ecstatic Beatles' fans.[11]

Also offering de-luxe homage is The Musical Box, a band which for ten years, has been re-creating the work of British band Genesis, restricting their repertoire solely to the original group's output between the years 1973–1975. Genesis enjoyed a cult following in their heyday and the Canadian tribute lovingly recreates the individual shows with dazzling accuracy. The Musical Box's concern for detail has fuelled a relentless search for archived images and films of Genesis as well as interviews with original crew members. They even managed to acquire the original Coral Sitar featured on the song, *I Know What I Like.* In a case of art mirroring life, their efforts to revive the period arrangements were eventually assisted by Genesis' very own keyboard maestro Tony Banks, who allowed them access to the original multi-track recordings. Their dedication eventually paid off and they have performed their work at prestigious venues such as the Albert Hall in London and The Olympia in Paris.

Full Tribute Case Study – The Counterfeit Stones

Founder member Steve Elson first saw The Rolling Stones on television in 1964, the year he began playing guitar. Portending a career as a tribute artist, his first school band won a holiday camp talent contest playing the Stones' number one record *It's All Over Now*. He graduated to a semi-professional band whilst at secondary school before going on to work for the legendary Arthur Howes agency.[12] From here he went on to work as a record plugger and publisher before moving eventually, into music production and management. A prototype Stones tribute, The Strolling Bones, was created with members of British pop band The Equals, whilst managing their tour in Zambia but it wasn't until he saw The Bootleg Beatles in concert, that Elson took the idea seriously and took a new version of The Strolling Bones on the road. Elson left the band in 1987 following an offer of record deal working with another Stones sound-alike band. Broken English's hit single *Coming On Strong* was widely assumed by the media to be a new Stones single, then, four years later The Counterfeit Stones (Figure 4.3) were formed for a one-off gig in America. As the groundwork to put on the show had involved a lot of hard work, they contacted a few agents and were soon offered bookings. Their current line up (2009) consists of Elson playing Nick Dagger, Bill Lennon as Keef Rickard, John Prynn as Charlie Mott. Bill Hymen is played by Alan Mian and the ubiquitous David Birnie is charged with the role of representing Byron Jones, Mick Taylor-Made and Ronnie B. Goode at different points during the show. The band also uses the services of Holger Skepeneit, who trebles up as Manfred Mann, Nicky Popkiss and Chuck Ravel.

Elements of humour, irony and musicianship are injected into their act in equal measures: at certain points in the performance, self-reflexivity is mobilized as the fictional nature of the illusion is exposed. There are sly references to Keith Richards' legendary drug intake and Mick Jagger's vanity and during costume changes the parody continues via short filmed sketches of major events in the Rolling Stones' career, such as the infamous Redlands drug bust of 1967 and the band's sullen appearance on mainstream television favourite, *Jukebox Jury* three years earlier.[13] In addition to a healthy schedule of corporate gigs, theatre shows and university balls, they have played private parties for Bill Clinton, Sir Tim Rice, Phil Collins and Princess Stephanie of Monaco amongst others. When combined with the length of their career, the fact that their shows continue to sell out, is a testimony to the Counterfeit's enduring popularity.

Sound-alike or Reverence Bands

Only a limited number of original bands have attracted full tributes, mainly because this type of act is much more expensive to establish; running costs

Figure 4.3 The Counterfeit Stones (photograph Steve Elson, by permission)

are higher and as already noted, not all musicians want to engage in identity impersonation anyway. The decision is also dependent on the original band's visual appeal, as Davis (2006: 845) points out, "There seems to be a correlation between the visual aspect of the original artist and whether the specialist cover band playing that artist's music falls into the reverence or tribute band category."[14] Those whose looks are forgettable, tend to be consigned to the less glamorous category of sound-alike. If we take the example of Steely Dan, a rock band, admired more for their music than their looks, imitators Nearly Dan and Stealing Dan make no attempts whatsoever to resemble their template, concentrating instead on reproducing the band's complex jazz influenced structures and harmonies.[15] Excessive emphasis on virtuosity has major financial implications though – imitators of the visually uninteresting such as Nearly Dan, can expect to earn considerably less than their more image conscious counterparts. The UK entertainment agency Alive Network's website,[16] reveals that cover and reverence bands generally earn far less than look-alike tributes which are capable of commanding in excess of £11,000 per booking. For full tributes, the rewards are higher still now that audiences have become increasingly sophisticated participants in what Baudrillard (1981) referred to as the "sign-economy." This is particularly so in the self-referential, media-infused world of popular music where appearances are everything. Giving some measure of the scale of the reward, Bjorn Again were recently paid £20,000 to perform at the Kremlin before Russian Prime Minister Vladimir Putin.[17]

In a world preoccupied with good looks, sound-alikes distinguish themselves in the semiotic supermarket by striving to promote musical integrity and the value of craftsmanship. Levels of musicianship do vary across the scene and whilst many Elvis impersonators offer entertainment in the broadest sense of the word, they do not necessarily need to be able to play a guitar or sing very well in order to amuse the audience, illustrating Shumaway's observation that: "The culture's interest in them is not in how they sing or play an instrument, but in their bringing to life the character Elvis Presley performed" (Shumway, in Horner and Swiss 2000: 197). Within the culture of rock music though, virtuosity and the ability to play convincingly are hallmarks of authenticity and the "miming Elvis" approach will not do. This explains the rock audience's acceptance of sound-alikes, whose failure to reconstruct identity is mitigated by their high calibre musicianship skills.

Those restricted by their unique physical attributes, may not be able to offer a credible resemblance either, and some are unable to tolerate the rigmarole of dressing in character. Steve Elson of the Counterfeit Stones said that certain musicians simply cannot wear wigs and few are able to maintain the skinny frame required to represent The Rolling Stones in the early years of their career (he admits to being a keep fit fanatic). Moreover, even if they are the right height or physique, they may object to impersonation for personal reasons.

Despite the fact that their prototype had one of the most dynamic and instantly recognizable images, the successful British band Whole Lotta Led, make no deliberate attempt to look like Led Zeppelin, their commitment to the representation of sound, is stated clearly on their website:

> Unlike the majority of bands on the tribute circuit, Whole Lotta Led are a sound-a-like as opposed to a look-a-like band. They believe that the music comes first and wearing wigs and costumes can distract from what they are trying to achieve – which is to play some of the best music ever written.[18]

This implies that their intentions are more seriously musicological than those of their rivals. It also suggests a rejection of the shallow lure of the visual over other sensory channels. When I discussed the subject of physical impersonation with the band, they said that they were unwilling to dress up like Zeppelin because they associated the whole idea of costumes with the cabaret circuit, something they wished to distance themselves from.

In other cases, the decision to avoid impersonation may reflect the character or ethos of the original band. Members of the original Pink Floyd did not present themselves as glamorous individuals, the emphasis on their show was somewhat impersonal, focusing less on individual identity and more on collective musicianship and the use of elaborate multi-media. A review of one of their shows emphasizes this point.

> The Pink Floyd members do not run around the stage like run-of-the-mill rock stars; they simply occupy the stage and provide the music while high-tech lighting, films, and dramatic effects tell their dark tales. The miniature airplane that crashes to the stage during "Dark Side of the Moon," the gigantic flying pig that buzzes the audience during "Animals," and the animated cartoons, particularly Gerald Scarfe's frightening accompaniment to"Welcome to the Machine," have provided some of the most memorable moments in Rock and Roll. (Williams 1988)

Taking a lead from the original band, The Australian Pink Floyd are similarly inclined. Steve Mac who performs Dave Gilmour's part, stresses the importance they place on the music: "There's no attempt to look like any of the Pink Floyd members themselves. We didn't get into it for that – we got into it for the music." Like their archetype, they rely instead, on visual effects, including a psychedelic lightshow modelled on the ones used by Pink Floyd in their 1987 and 1994 world tours.[19]

Sound-alike Case Study – Whole Lotta Led

Whole Lotta Led were formed in 1996. They are currently the UK's only full time professional Led Zeppelin tribute and their aim is "to reproduce the classic Zep songs with the same enthusiasm, excitement and passion" as the original group (wholelottaled.co.uk). Guitarists and founder members Geoff Hunt and Nick Ferris played together in another band during the 1980s. Ferris had seen Led Zeppelin at The Bath Blues Festival in 1969 and Hunt became a fan after his sister bought him their second album. Originally working under the name No Quarter, the band started out as a rock outfit, performing a generic repertoire of covers, interspersed with the odd original composition. They also included a limited number of Led Zeppelin numbers in their sets and, since these received a particularly enthusiastic response, they made the decision to change their name and stick to Zeppelin music solely. Drummer Graham Twist and lead singer Lee Addison joined the current line up in response to an advert. Twist, an alumnus of Drum Tech in London discovered Led Zeppelin when a friend introduced him to their film *The Song Remains the Same* while Addison was inspired initially by a school music teacher.

Figure 4.4 Whole Lotta Led (photograph Graham Twist, by permission)

Although Whole Lotta Led make no deliberate attempt to look like their archetypes, Addison does bear more than a fleeting resemblance to a young Robert Plant and in terms of dress sensibility, the band's wardrobe connotes a hint of 1960s, dressed-down chic (Figure 4.4). Major investment in sound reproduction is signalled by the lengthy and detailed list of each artist's equipment on their website.

List of Nick Ferris's Equipment

- Marshall EL34 100/100 stereo power amp
- 2 × Marshall JCM 900 lead 1960 4 × 12 stereo cabs
- 2 × Marshall JMP1 pre-amps
- Mesa Boogie 2:90 power amp (spare)
- Rocktron stereo rack mount effects
- Intellifex and Replifex units
- Gibson Les Paul Standard '59 Jimmy Page signature model (serial no Page 053) – Tom Murphy aged, based on Jimmy Page's #1 guitar
- Gibson Twin Neck guitar
- Gibson Les Paul Standard '58 reissue guitar (2001 model)
- Gibson Les Paul Standard '59 reissue guitar (2003 model) Ex Mick Ralphs of Bad Company
- Gibson SG special guitar (1968 model)
- Fender Jazzmaster guitar (1959 model)
- PRS custom ten top birds guitar
- Schecter Strat Dream Machine guitar (1984 model)
- Taylor acoustic guitar
- Behringer midi effects board
- Boss wah wah pedal

Source: www.wholelottaled.co.uk/nick_ferris.html (accessed July 2009).

After a spell playing pubs and small clubs, the band gravitated to larger rock venues and theatres in the UK and Europe. They can perform around three quarters of the Zeppelin repertoire and their two and a half hour set always includes the classics: *Moby Dick*, *Whole Lotta Love* and *Stairway to Heaven*. Aside from their musical connection to Led Zeppelin, the band also raises money for The ABC Trust, a charitable organization founded by Jimmy Page's wife.[20]

The Best of Both Worlds – Look and Sound-Alikes

The majority of acts do not make an either/or choice between sound and image, opting instead, to provide a halfway house reflecting their personal preferences and limitations. Some concession to resemblance offers a sensory cue for the audience to fill in the gaps and if the lead vocalist looks all right, fans will usually let their imagination do the rest. In Roxy Magic, a band which pays tribute to both Roxy Music and Bryan Ferry, the lead singer Kevin Hackett, was fortunate enough to be in possession of the winning combination – a voice remarkably similar to Ferry's and a striking physical likeness to the man – a resemblance exploited through careful attention to both dress and performance style. In the words of fellow band member Lee Sullivan,

> Our singer dresses in white tuxedo and sharp suits and resembles Bryan Ferry quite closely; he has studied Ferry over the years and uses mannerisms and stage moves that are very "Ferryesque." His voice has a natural similarity of timbre which he has refined to complete the impersonation. (Lee Sullivan, email, March 2007)

The rest of the band does not strive for impersonation and Sullivan added that, as he did not bear any physical resemblance to Roxy Music's Andy Mackay, he simply wears a stage outfit similar to one worn by his hero. Emphasizing the gravity of their role in interpreting Roxy Music's repertoire, he said the band chose not to parody the original artists' names because, in his words: "We do not use amusing 'alter ego' stage names as many tribute bands do – it was felt from early on that, although we do have fun on stage, that a humorous approach wouldn't suit the Roxy image."

Jack of All Trades – the Generalists

While the musicians studied so far, use their in-depth knowledge to recreate the work of a particular band, other performers are charged with the contrasting problem of offering breadth and variety. Specificity is not necessarily an advantage for entertainers since, although there is a likely audience for most tributes to an individual artist or band, the narrow repertoire which ignites passion in one context will alienate anyone who didn't like the music in the first place. For example, only the brave or foolhardy would book a Motörhead or Sex Pistols tribute for the average wedding reception, bar-mitzvah or engagement party, where the age range and mood of the event would normally preclude such wild risk-taking. Certain events cry out for the services of a generalist and this is where cover bands and generic tributes come into their own. By offering a broad spectrum, they reverse the logic of Mies van der Rohe's famous dictum that "Less is More," since for any band aiming to please the middle-of the-road audience, the emphasis must be on variety. Generalists appear regularly at end-of-the-pier shows, Christmas parties and corporate functions and are equally popular on cruise ships and at stag or hen nights.

In order to do each artist justice, polymorphic tributes make use of a hotch-potch of signifiers, designed to conjure up the spirit, rather than the letter of the era in question. They generally feature a backing band and one or two lead singers whose job it is to give the audience a snapshot of the genre or decade they represent. This requires judicious use of wigs, make up and rapid fire costume changes: the pressure on the singers is intense since it is they, more than the backing musicians who are charged with embodying the disparate range of characters. To accomplish this, they must have tremendous energy as well as sufficient acting ability to reproduce in quick succession, the mannerisms, dance moves and vocal styles of well-known pop stars. The '80s Experience ubiquitous stage show, incorporates the work of up to 20 artists, all enacted within a 45 minute slot. Over the past ten years, the group have performed worldwide, sometimes working alongside notable alumni of the 1980s such as the New Pop icons Tony Hadley of Spandau Ballet and Martin Fry of ABC. Although they provide a more versatile form of entertainment than the likes of Whole Lotta Led or Bjorn Again, generalists are distinctive enough to differentiate themselves within the marketplace from their predecessors, the cover groups. However despite their more elaborate efforts to simulate the music of various artists, their function is broadly similar because it seems that audiences still enjoy the social experience of dancing to live pop music, especially at intergenerational get-togethers.

Playing with Identity: The Transgender Tributes

Leaving aside arguments concerning the relative importance of image versus sound and moving next to the politics of the personal, it would be fair to say that the vast majority of mainstream tributes do little to challenge gender stereotyping. In cultivating and feeding nostalgia, particularly its tendency to react to temporal dislocation and the inevitability of the future with either sentimentality or resistance to change, they avoid progress and any radical tendencies towards reform. On the surface, their replication of the status quo only serves to reinforce existing structural inequalities such as the hegemony of masculinity in rock and metal music already documented by Frith and McRobbie (1978), Walser (1993) and Weinstein (1991).

Taking this into account, it is interesting to note that a growing minority of female musicians is now finding employment playing rock homage but if they are to catch up with their male counterparts, they have a long way to go! Reinholtz (1991) found that of the top 20 popular songs between 1956 and 1990, 71 per cent were performed by male artists and in the Rock and Roll Hall of Fame's "500 songs that shaped popular music," only 35 of the songs listed, were recorded by female artists.[21] Explanations for the under-representation of female musicians is provided by Bayton (1998) whose work uncovered a range of factors mitigating against women's active participation in rock. These included lack of access to leisure time and transport, family commitments, the masculine coding of certain instruments and genres, fear of technology, institutionalized sexism and peer group pressure. Furthermore, research undertaken by Chesky and Corns (1999: 14) demonstrates that even when they do secure employment as musicians, women can expect to earn less than their male counterparts.

I was interested to find a growing number of cross-gender groups reversing this dismal trend, with female musicians paying homage to male hard rock and heavy metal bands of the 1970s and 1980s. The groups are located primarily in the US and their number includes the San Francisco and Seattle based tributes to AC/DC – AC/She and Hell's Belles; Los Angeles tribute to Iron Maiden – The Iron Maidens and the New York band, Lez Zeppelin, who bring to life, the work of Led Zeppelin. These bands disrupt traditional gender discourses by challenging the assumed heterosexual address of the original performance thereby confronting what Meyer (1994) refers to as, "the cultural products of the straight mind."[22] They also showcase the talent of the female musicians which might otherwise go unnoticed as working in an all-female group provides advantages which allow women to overcome the obstacles normally excluding them from active participation in rock music.[23] According to Wanda Ortiz, The Iron Maidens (Figure 4.5) work together in a co-operative fashion to allow members to cope with issues regarding childcare – a major problem for most female musicians.

> We have had a few mothers in the band ... We always worked it out though. Currently, only our singer is a mother with a teenage son so it's not that big of a problem for us. The rest of us are willing to work things out so she can be in the band and take care of her family. For example, if that means not taking a gig so she can see her son graduate from high school, then that's okay with us. I'm sure it's still a challenge for her to find a good balance but I think we all realize that and do what we can to help out. (Wanda Ortiz, email, May, 2007)

Another advantage of an all-female band, is that women are able to explore their virtuosity and develop greater confidence in performance skills without being subjected to sexist strategies of bullying and marginalization.

Despite their all-female status, their appeal is not limited to a feminine fan base: Iron Maidens' Aja Kim said that the majority of their audience consists of males aged between 13 and 45, who come to see the band out of curiosity or to confirm their belief that women are incapable of playing hard and heavy rock music. Their response is generally positive but several of the female musicians I spoke to confirmed that the boisterous and sexist behaviour of male fans could be problematic. The male fascination with female bands is not entirely rooted in heterosexual fantasies however. These acts also allows men to engage with the repressed feelings of desire they may have experienced

Figure 4.5 The Iron Maidens (photograph Wanda Ortiz, by permission)

while watching the erotically charged performances of male rock and heavy metal frontmen, According to Sedgwick (1985) the parameters of same sex relationships are often blurred and between men, potential arises for a homosocial bond, a connection fuelled ultimately by desire.[24] Due to the hegemony of heterosexuality, the libidinal force of the male audience's response to female tributes may be attributed to the release of hitherto unexpressed emotions. In this sense, their passionate outpouring reverses the conventional view of rock's gendered spectatorship where:

> All sexual desire is seen from feminine fan perspective and male sexual desire is repressed. The sexualised female spectator thus serves as a figurehead for all sexual desire and provides an outlet for the sexual underpinning of the event. The spectacular nature of her image masks other sexual desires and renders them invisible. (Fonarow 2006: 207)

The transgender bands' queer interpretation of the work of the male rock icons creates the "gender trouble" identified by Butler (1990) in her critique of identity politics. By problematizing fixed notions of what it is to be male or female and through their critique of essentialism, female tributes use embodiment to expose the constructed nature of genre's masculinity. As Butler writes:

> In imitating gender, drag implicitly reveals the imitative structure of gender itself – as well as its contingency. Indeed, part of the pleasure, the giddiness of the performance is in the recognition of a radical contingency in the relation between sex and gender in the face of cultural configurations of causal unities that are regularly assumed to be natural and necessary. (Butler 1990: 137–138)

This subversion of the traditional male heterosexual address and performance, invites differing audience perspectives, allowing anyone who wants to be transformed by the music to join in and participate in whatever way they choose. In Steph Paynes of Lez Zeppelin's words, "We get all sorts. Twelve year old kids and their parents who saw Led Zep play in 1974. We get guys, girls, and gays of all kinds. It's a completely eclectic crowd, but everyone has one thing in common, and that's a mutual adoration of Led Zeppelin" (Steph Paynes, email March 2007). The band's version of the orgasmic anthem *Whole Lotta Love*, positions women at the epicentre of sexual expressiveness, making them the perpetrators rather than the recipients of the inflated carnal promises of the male protaganists. This is a reversal of the natural order of heavy rock, where the relationship between musician and instrument, traditionally led to, "musical skills becom[ing] equated with sexual skills" and "'cock rockers' ... using their instruments to 'show what they've got'" (Frith: 1978).

Regardless of their ability, there is pressure on female musicians to prove that they are as good as their male counterparts. For a convincing performance, instruments must be played with sufficient levels of power and strength and the correct volume and tone of the male voice needs to be matched as closely as possible. Audiences are often shocked when they discover that women really can play hard rock, as Aja Kim explains:

> We get a lot of people who can't believe women are playing this music and who have their doubts initially that we can pull it off. Once they experience our show the doubts dissolve and they completely accept and respect us, because they see and hear that we are serious musicians with serious chops who are also fans and love this music as much as they do. (Aja Kim, email, March 2004)

Case Study: Lez Zeppelin

Lez Zeppelin were formed in New York during 2003 to perform the work of Led Zeppelin, a group renowned for the power and intensity of their hard rock, fused with an eclectic mixture of folk and other genres. The original Zeppelin's career ended abruptly following the untimely death of drummer John Bonham in 1980 and subsequently the band's repertoire has become a classic text for imitative performance. Lez Zep did not set out to trade on the novelty factor of their femininity, they came together in response to lead guitarist Steph Payne's enduring passion for Zeppelin's music. Since its inception the band's original line-up has evolved and at the time or writing, Leesa-Harrington Squyres accompanies Payne as their John Bonham, Megan Thomas plays bass guitar, keyboards and mandolin and singer Shannon Conley fronts the band as lead vocalist (Figure 4.6).

Figure 4.6 Lez Zeppelin (photograph Steph Paynes, by permission)

Their clever choice of name with its inferences of Sapphic love has created endless speculation about band members' sexuality. The fact that they refuse to admit or refute charges of lesbianism only fuels media curiosity. Within a genre defined by discourses of male heterosexual freedom where a masculinist performance style dominates, this definitely/maybe response (regardless of whether or not it is a calculated move to attract publicity), creates a certain mystique which simply heightens the band's appeal Lez Zeppelin's career has progressed from playing small gigs in and around New York to playing before a crowd of 40,000 in Times Square and touring across Europe. In 2007, they were invited to play at the three day Download Festival in the UK and the same year they played the prestigious Bonnaroo Festival in Tennessee where ironically, Robert Plant was also performing with the bluegrass artist Alison Krause.

Male Transgender Tributes

Alongside the rapidly expanding list of female rock acts, there are a very limited number of male transgender tributes to female pop icons and girl groups. In choosing pop, male performers are simply reversing the conventional industry dynamic of a genre dominated by female artists. Greig (1989) for example, identifies girl bands as one of the central traditions in mainstream pop music where female artists do, at least, have a track record of success. The female artists who are imitated tend to have larger-than-life onstage personalities, making them a natural target for impersonators. Like the stereotypical female icons of gay culture, they seem to be chosen for their combination of glamour, flamboyance and strength. Examples include homages to pop group The Go Go's (The Ga Ga's), Madonna (We Got The Meat and Mandonna) and The Dixie Chicks (Chicks with Dixies).

The male dance troupe Mandonna, pay homage to the ever-changing pop princess in, what is described on their website as an "Alpha Male tribute to the Material Girl." The seven piece band are not female impersonators: their bearded frontman makes no effort to disguise his gender and all sing in the natural male bass and tenor vocal range. Within stage shows, they take full advantage of Madonna's sensational wardrobe and onstage dance routines, making more than ten costume changes to show off 20 years of cutting edge fashions (these include the wedding gown worn in *Like a Virgin* as well as her trademark pointed bustier of the 1980s). According to bass player Charlie Moto, the audience at their Mandonna show includes a mixture of gay men, middle-aged women and older Madonna fans although more recently, they have started to see teenagers at gigs.

Mandonna's camp performance could be viewed as an ironic investigation of femininity, playing heavily on the existing associations of gay men with disco as well as Madonna's cult status as a dance diva within the gay community.[25] Whether or not it parodies overblown femininity, in common with the majority of male tributes to female artists, Mandonna's performance veers towards the deliberately clumsy, and the emphasis is on humour. Efforts to represent femininity are achieved more through elaborate costume changes, exaggerated haute "feminine" gestures and camp dance routines in a performance style which contrasts sharply with the blank parody used by females in homages to male icons. Rather than critiquing patriarchy, the absurd posturing connotes misogyny, illustrating Robertson's (1996: 142) observations concerning camp's potential to affirm patriarchy and marginalize the feminine. Arguing that while, "Camp may appropriate and expose stereotypes," she makes the points that "it also in some measure, keeps them alive." This is achieved through the contradictory forces of camp which allow it to act as both "a mode of excess" or "a mode of containment." Thus, rather than representing the strength of Madonna's femininity, the band ridicules and undermine it.

Confronting Classification – the Cross Genre Tributes

Whereas transgender tributes comment upon dominant narratives of gender or sexuality, cross-genre acts provide a similar function in critiquing the limitations of genre boundaries. Genre's role as a fundamental organizing tool is well established in both academic and industry circles. As Shuker (1994) explains, genres are clearly defined and recognized by music retailers, marketing managers and fans alike, influencing everything from the layout of music stores to the content of competing radio stations. Moreover, as Hartley (1994: 128) contends, in their role as "agents of ideological closure," genres have the power to "limit the meaning potential of a given text," a quality which allows the industry to police and predict patterns of consumption. Cross-genre tributes challenge these genre conventions for, unlike signed artists who must follow the record industry rules, they are able to take far greater risks and as a consequence, can offer some of the most inventive texts. This is achieved by playing around with the elements which normally constitute a genre or by deliberately flaunting the established rules: typically, the approach is light-hearted but there are examples of more serious attempts to sabotage categorization.

The approach of Dread Zeppelin, a band originating from Pasadena, epitomizes the adventurous spirit of the non-conformists. Formed in 1989 and fronted by an Elvis impersonator, they play reggae versions of Led Zeppelin classics, fusing previously disparate elements in a creative mish-mash. At an artistic level, the intermingling of Presley's hit *Heartbreak Hotel* with Zeppelin's classic *Heartbreaker*, might seem a little incongruous but, from the point of view of dismantling the hyperbolic aura surrounding the original text, Dread Zeppelin succeed in inviting new ways of engaging with the music. The introduction of humour and chaos within the performance counteracts the excessive reverence normally directed towards Led Zeppelin, allowing a decidedly carnivaleque atmosphere to emerge. In their subversion of usual assumptions connoted by the genres, they challenge some of the more predictable responses to a classic text.

Other interesting hybrids are, The Duke of Uke, a ukulele player famed for his Sex Pistols covers and Schlong, a now defunct Californian band which created an epic punk version of the Bernstein's classic *West Side Story*. Pairings like these are certainly unexpected – their imaginative reconfiguration of previously unrelated genres and texts opens up potential for the creation of new and unexpected meanings. The use of the ukulele, brings humour to a genre of music normally linked to anger and youthful agit-prop, and in doing so, provides an alternative to angst for angst's sake. This playful approach may not endear the majority but in exposing popular music's tendency to take itself a little too seriously, it offers a refreshing antidote to reverentiality.[26]

Perhaps because of the genre's camp theatricality (heavily satirized in the 1984 'mockumentary' *This is Spinal Tap)*, metal lends itself more readily to parody than other styles and the metal convention of exaggerated virtuosity somehow invites caricature and quotation. Whatever the reasons, attempts to blend metal with other less jarring styles, abound. Hayseed Dixie (cheekily named after rock gods AC/DC), are an interesting cross-genre group which, like other "genre benders," plays games with heavy metal by mixing the metal sound with bluegrass (Figure 4.7). As they cover some of the classic rock texts, replacing the screech of the electric guitar with twanging banjos, the incongruous concoction of rock and country is delivered without a hint of irony Although the cocktail shouldn't work, the end product is strangely spirited and uplifting, with the metal anthems acting as an ideal antidote to country music's mawkish tendencies, while the lighter tones of bluegrass smooth away the rawness and rougher edges of the original songs.

Musical matchmaking like this, is not confined solely to popular music genres – there are other instances of unusual pairing. The work of Black Sabbath has been reinterpreted by an Estonian early music group, Rondellus, an ensemble whose quest for the authentic compelled them to translate the original lyrics into Latin. Many would recoil in horror at the union, but producer Mikhel Raud had no difficulties in identifying the virtues of this potentially awkward marriage, arguing that: "There is a strong connection, musically, and if you think of heavy metal in general, the symbolism they use is very medieval."[27] In another fascinating fusion of classical and rock, The Finnish group Apocalyptica play heavy metal on the cello. Along with a drummer, the graduates of the Sibelius Academy in Helsinki, created the album *Apocalyptica: Plays Metallica by Four Cellos* (1996). The record may not have flown off the shelves of music stores but there is more than a passing interest in these oddball marriages.

Figure 4.7 Hayseed Dixie (photograph Free Trade Agency, by permission)

The icons of heavy metal, Metallica, are subjected to the largest share of genre engineering experiments. Metabbalism, a Welsh band, blends their distinctive sound with Abba's classic pop harmonies while the New York group Tragedy, match the power of heavy metal with The Bee Gees's pop ballads. By far the most adventurous though, are Beatallica, a US group which fuses the words and music of The Beatles and Metallica, to a point where it is almost impossible to separate one from the other. What drives the musicians involved, to undertake these odd experiments in the first place? Every case is different but for Metabbalism, the break with musical convention appears to have happened more by accident than design. Band representative Matthew told me the idea for the project emerged when two of his friends were performing a cover of ABBA's *Does Your Mother Know* in the style of a version recorded by rock band Ash. This in turn led him to reflect upon the potential of further forays across the genre boundaries.

> I was inspired – so were the audience – how many more songs of Abba's could be "tampered" with in rock fashion? In short, lots! Any act I was to put together had to break away from the usual straight forward two male, two female fronted Abba acts – it needed to be a full band line up. That's when my train of thought ran away ... Abba, rock-band, kitsch, metal, kitsch, metal ... camp, heavy metal ... Judas Priest, '80s hair metal, Spinal Tap, Bon Jovi ... And so on, the imagery was all in place – have the band dress up in leather, lace, spandex, hair has to be bubble perms and mullets. A tribute to ABBA and a tribute to metal – best of both worlds. (Matthew, email August 2004)

Beatallica – a Cross-Genre Case Study

Metabbalism do at least, maintain the integrity of the original text but Beatallica's complex, synthesis of heavy metal and pop challenges authorship just as much as it confronts genre boundaries. Beatallica are not really a tribute band, they prefer to describe their work as a live "mash-up," an approach which involves combining fragments of the music and lyrics of The Beatles to those of Metallica, to which they then add their own lyrics, and just to complicate things further, they make changes to the original tempo, key and time signatures (Figure 4.8). The Beatles classic hit *Let it Be* when fused with Metallica's *The Thing That Should Not B*, becomes *The Thing That Should Not Let it Be* and in the same manner, Beatallica's *And Justice for all My Loving*, draws on the metal anthem *And Justice for All* with the pop classic *All My Loving.*

Krk Hammetson and singer Jaymz Lennfield initiated the project in 2001 by creating the CD *A Garage Dayz Nite* to commemorate the annual Spoof Fest concert held in Milwaukee. A limited number of the CDs were given to festival-goers and a web page including MP3 versions of the songs was subsequently created by a fan. The name Beatallica was given to the group by a Milwaukee internet radio presenter, but the band were unaware of these activities, or of the fan following which the page had generated until 2002, when they met its creator. After giving their seal of approval to the webpage, Beatallica responded to requests for more material by releasing an eponymous EP (also known as *The Grey Album*) in 2004. With a drummer and bass player, Beatallica put together a stage show which, like their recordings, blends aspects of both The Beatles and Metallica's live performances. The current line up of Jaymz Lennfield (lead vocals, rhythm guitar), Krk Hammetson (lead guitar), Kliff McBurtney (bass, backing vocals) and Ringo Larz (drums), and their most

Figure 4.8 Beatallica (photograph Michael Tierney, by permission)

recent offering, an official debut, is the album *Sgt. Hetfield's Motorbreath Pub Band.* Beatallica's work clearly transcends simple imitation – song lyrics make satirical allusions to important themes within the metal community (such as maintaining the purity of the genre or ridding the genre of Glam Metal softies) and the band make comic references to the heavy beer drinking habits of the metal community in "mash-ups" which use high levels of imagination, musicianship and judgement.

Confronting Anything and Everything – File Under Miscellaneous Mayhem

Certain tributes, due to determination to push established boundaries of taste and convention, simply defy any form of categorization The cross-genre bands explored thus far appear mildly eccentric when their efforts are compared to those of the tribute scene's avant-garde. Would anyone, in their wildest dreams, envisage a musical collaboration between Elvis Presley, Bob Marley and Joy Division? Belfast tribute artist Jimmy the King, accompanied by The Questionnaires, undertakes the challenging experiment of performing songs associated with artists other than Presley, while delivering them in the King's inimicable style. Included in the repertoire are Presleyesque versions of Bob Marley's *No Woman No Cry* and Joy Division's *Love Will Tear Us Apart.*[28]

Another "extreme" tribute is offered by The Misfats who, billed as "The World's Fattest Misfits Cover Band," parody the work of the 1970s punk rockers, The Misfits – a collective famed for their fusion of horror film with punk rock. The Misfats parodic commentary on body fascism is achieved through a revision of the Misfits' original lyrics to reflect upon the contemporary obsession with food and appetite. For example the line "*I got something to say ... I killed a baby today*" from Misfits' song *Last Caress* (1997) is transformed into "I got something to say ... I ate a baby today!" and retitled *Last Carcass.* On the surface this may appear to be little more than tasteless satire, but at a deeper level, the band's guerrilla textual practices highlight popular culture's power to expose the inconsistencies and irrationalities of mainstream discourses. The work of the Misfats articulates the agony of the obese, in a culture which condones excessive consumption providing a skeletal frame is maintained.

Other tributes confront unhealthier aspects of the mythology surrounding rock and pop, a task carried out very effectively, by the school age imitators of iconic rock and metal bands. Guns and Roses are parodied by the child tribute, Li'l G'n'R; Toddler Metallica who pay homage to Metallica and The Red Hot Mini Peppers and Tiny Mötley Crüe represent juvenile versions of The Red Hot Chile Peppers and Mötley Crüe. According to their manager the five piece Li'l G'n'R, was assembled following an audition of over 100 children. Those selected, on the basis of their "rock star mentality" and the desire to party, were offered scaled-down versions of original instruments and despite being put together as a gimmick, they have played several sell out concerts. Although undeniably cute, there is something deeply disturbing about children performing songs about rock's darker world of sex and drugs, death and destruction. Their assumed innocence automatically prompts reflection upon the genre's narrow obsession with carnal love and drug addled oblivion at the expense of healthier mind expansion and less overtly sexualized attachments![29]

My final example must also be the most preposterous. In a world informed by mimicry it was only a matter of time before someone created a tribute to a parody. Inspired by the need to find an antidote to the earnestness of official Beatles' conventions and despite being staunch fans themselves, The Yellow SubMorons founding members decided it was time to inject a little fun into these events, to offset the earnest atmosphere at play-offs. Their solution was the creation of a homage to the British parody band, The Rutles! Perhaps more than anything, acts like these show that popular culture, far from being devoid of significance and unable to make use of recognizable aesthetic processes, is more than capable of rigorous interrogation of its own output. Artificial binaries between high and low culture, only establish a false hierarchy of worth which identifies standardization and degradation in products designed for popular consumption. The fans and performers of the tribute scene exercise very acute judgement and taste, and are just as aware of distinctions in value as any opera, ballet or theatre lover.

5 Getting Established and Maintaining a Career

Letz Zep, Stairway to Zeppelin, Led by Zeppelin or indeed, any of the others dedicated to performing Led Zeppelin's work are unlikely to attract an audience of 20,000 as the original band did in 2007.[1] Tributes to the mighty Zeppelin are not going to ascend the stairway to rock heaven and be inducted into the Rock and Roll Hall of Fame either. Not only are the financial rewards for their efforts modest but the work is hard too: Bob Dylan's impressive total of around 100 appearances a year in "The Never Ending Tour," is a mere drop in the musical ocean when compared to the punishing schedules endured by the more successful tribute acts.[2] In contrast with their original counterparts, parodic entertainers do not have to spend months working feverishly on the creation of a new repertoire since theirs is already established. They do though, face other challenges. Without the prospect of a growing body of recordings and royalties, they can never escape from the stresses and strains of touring in a working life, which for successful acts, can consist of playing live shows for up to two-thirds of the year. No mean feat when staying in budget hotels and travelling considerable distances in less than luxurious transport. Furthermore, maintaining the enthusiasm to play someone else's material year in year out, can lead to creative frustration and the desire to break free. The typical tensions which prevail in any group of musicians are magnified significantly for those who must spend so much of their time together. These trials and tribulations are further heightened by the constant pressure of intense competition which characterizes the world of budget entertainment. In this chapter the working life of musicians who earn a living from paying homage will be explored in an effort to illustrate how they climb a career ladder to work as members of closely knit teams in a competitive industry. I will show how many of the top tribute artists are equipped the key skills beloved by employers in the modern marketplace. These skilled musicians confound the stereotype of the tribute artist as failed musicians, living in a fantasy world. In fact, the majority of those I encountered are highly motivated, versatile and personable individuals who demonstrate a very professional approach.

Due to the pre-eminence of certain discourses, we are encouraged to believe that life on the road is characterized by a combination of freedom, excitement, immoral excess and financial reward. The ironic take on life as a rock musician in The Byrds' record, *So You Want to be a Rock and Roll Star* (1967) where, provided "your hair [is] combed right and your pants fit tight, it's gonna be alright," enunciates a popular fantasy of a world we only gain access to through a complex system of mediation which strives to conceal the everyday realities of working in the music industry. The icons of rock and pop are portrayed as liberated individuals, freed from the humdrum demands of family life and the other dreary pressures endured by lesser mortals hence, to all intents and purposes, "the musician is seen as a free and creative spirit having little to do with the 9–5 routine" (Burton 2005: 169). Academic studies which might offer a more objective perspective are in short supply as there is limited coverage of the popular music apprenticeship or the working life of semi-professional rock and pop musicians. So far, the texts devoted to music-making tend to be restricted either by geographical or genre specificity. Examples include Bennett's (1980) examination of local music making (which concentrates on the career path of rock musicians in the US state of Colorado) and Cohen's (1991) study of rock music making which is centred on the local scene in Liverpool. Other studies such as Weinstein's (2000) investigation into the specific skills and competencies of artists operating within the heavy metal genre, and Finnegan's (1989) research on the varied, and sometimes interlocking music scenes in the Buckinghamshire town of Milton Keynes, are similarly restricted. When it comes to the everyday working lives of those who work predominantly within the live sector, the situation is exacerbated. Negus (2001) contends that there is a major shortage of research on the corps of musicians who make up the amateur and semi-professional sector. Furthermore, there are problems in locating accurate information about this under-researched workforce. Most of the artists are self-employed and the majority of bands operate as independent enterprises in an environment loosely organized around small scale clubs, pubs and theatres, where data is hard to come by.[3]

Starting Out: a Rock Education or an Apprenticeship?

How and why do musicians join tribute or cover bands, and what are their typical career paths? Do their working lives differ significantly from those of signed artists and if so, in what respects? None of the musicians I interviewed admitted to wanting to play an instrument with the sole intention of joining a tribute act, so we must suppose that this was not their original aim. However, in order to work within the budget end of the live sector they still had to acquire key skills. Getting a tribute on the road and making a living from it requires a combination of capabilities – musical and business oriented, which must be gained, either through formal education or alternatively, on the job. When it comes to the musical aspect, schools and higher education providers nowadays offer elements of music tuition, but for those born immediately after the war, there were no university or college courses in popular music. This situation though, is gradually changing and would-be musicians can choose now from a wide range of post-16 programmes. These courses aim to encourage individuals to explore their creativity while learning about the practicalities of a career in the music business and for this reason, course tutors are often experienced practitioners who can provide insights into current trends within the industry.[4] Although the practical and vocational content of these programmes challenges the traditional "art for art's sake" perspective on creativity, there are some impressive success stories. The Brit School in Croydon, for example, helped to launch the careers of Grammy award winning vocal artist Amy Winehouse, indie bands, The Feeling and The Kooks and the internationally successful R&B artist Leona Lewis is another alumnus.

Attendance at a high-profile performing arts school doesn't necessarily guarantee success though, for, as one observer points out, of those who do attend, "only a tiny minority of students will achieve fame as it is commonly understood."[5] This observation was confirmed by a college tutor and musician, with 15 years' experience of teaching popular music:

> I can only recall one student achieving serious fame and success, and it had nothing to do with the course! He left early following a successful audition with a manufactured boy band. I still cringe when I recall telling him he was making a massive mistake and he should stick with his course. A few months later he and his band had charted – a number one I think.
>
> The important point here though, is that when we interview and audition for the courses, we would be being incredibly irresponsible if we even hinted that that level of success is just around the corner. In fact, my approach is to say it is highly unlikely, but the course can provide a fantastic opportunity to develop a whole set of skills, that will (provided they work their backsides off), help them to earn a living within a massive and diverse industry. As for the beach house in Malibu, and a bevvy of Californian models (male or female!) at their beck and call? The lottery is statistically, probably a better bet. (Richard Longden, interview March 2009)

Popular music courses may be increasing in number but notwithstanding their availability, and despite the fact that research (Chesky and Corns 1999), indicates that college-trained musicians have greater earning potential than their uneducated counterparts, "learning by doing" still appears to be the norm. Only a minority of the musicians I interviewed had studied music to graduate level and beyond. Skills, it seems are normally acquired in a much more ad-hoc manner. and according to the majority, the typical route into a band included learning with friends, taking lessons here and there, developing a repertoire of covers while working on original compositions where time allows. In common with other crafts, a level of proficiency is required and for musicians, the ability to play an instrument with confidence is a key stage in the acquisition of performance skills. Some began to master these skills during childhood, giving them a head start: indeed, a striking quality shared by members of the most successful tribute acts, was an early commitment to a musical career. As Danielz, frontman of the internationally successful T Rex-stasy explains the importance of well-developed skills:

> One must first learn one's craft – like in any job, the better you learn it the more successful you could be. I was learning my craft since I was 14 years old, and that's why I do it as second nature. (Danielz, email, 7 July 2007)

Lee Addison, lead vocalist of Whole Lotta Led, told me that in his case, inspiration came from a music teacher who introduced him to Led Zeppelin's *Lemon Song* at the age of fourteen. Steve Elson of The Counterfeit Stones was another who honed core skills at a tender age and it wasn't long before his precocious talent was recognized:

> I first saw the Stones on TV in 1964. Just started learning guitar – and with my first kid band won a talent competition playing the Stones' first number 1, *It's All Over Now*. This was before my voice broke and made for a very weird Jagger impression but it went down a storm with the holiday camp audience! From then on I played in a semi-pro band during my grammar school years. I was even asked to qualify the lyrics of *Paint It Black* to the whole English class by the master who was teaching poetry and until my analysis had considered pop lyrics crass. He was converted. (Steve Elson, interview, September 2007)

Building a Porfolio of Skills

Mastering an instrument and the art of performance are clearly fundamental, but other capabilities are needed in the portfolio of competencies. Musicians must use many skills in a band, from learning to work as team players, managing their time effectively and making business decisions, to networking, budgeting, marketing and record keeping. Although professional management services are available, I found that quite a few successful tribute bands preferred to self-manage, running the act along similar lines to the small creative enterprises studied by Leadbeater and Oakley (1999: 24–25), whose research uncovered very distinctive characteristics amongst those working in the cultural industries. In addition to a notable tendency to operate with an independent ethos, the study identified a model of work similar to that of self-managing musicians. The research found a strong emphasis on self-reliance, a blurring of the distinctions between work and non-work as well as an ability to combine individualistic values with collaborative working across the wider creative community.

Looking at these points individually – collaboration between individuals ensures a broad mix of skills These are needed in cover or tribute bands, where many talents are pooled to make the enterprise work to the greatest advantage, particularly in the case of self-managing bands which must organize everything, from securing and advertising gigs, arranging transport and accommodation, to sorting out their own accounts, tax and insurance. The most successful musicians also utilize strong networking skills to make effective use of collaborators within the wider creative community, accepting the importance of competition, while promoting co-operation where necessary to achieve individual, as well as mutual goals. By joining forces in this way, they are able to exchange information on venues, share equipment, work together on mutually beneficially projects and provide support for one another in emergencies.[6]

Once basic skills have been mastered, a stint playing in either an original or a covers band is the next stage for the average musician. Aspiring original artists are keen to spend as little time possible on this rung of the ladder but pop biographies demonstrate quite clearly, that it cannot be avoided. The majority of famous performers played covers during the early years of their careers since it takes time to develop a repertoire of original material.[7] Having gained the pre-requisite ability to work in a professional manner, original bands will try to perform their own material where possible. This may be incorporated by way of a compromise, into a set of covers or, in the case of the more intransigent, original work will form the entire repertoire. The chances of securing a reliable audience, let alone a record deal are slim, as there are far more musicians looking for regular employment than there are career opportunities available.[8] Those fortunate enough to secure a contract will find themselves reliant on the services of other industry professionals since, as Frith (2001) observes, creativity alone is not sufficient to guarantee a successful career as a musician.

> individual artists and performers are rarely in a position themselves to get their work to the public. They need to contract other people – agents, promoters, publishers, record companies – to organise and promote concert tours, to manufacture scores and records and CDs. (Frith 2001: 49)

Musicians on the tribute scene will carry out many of these tasks themselves. They cannot depend on an income generated from record sales which means that their success is almost entirely dependent on their ability to secure regular bookings and to maintain a fan base. For these reasons, successful outfits are invariably fronted by highly motivated, time-served, professionals who have the superior technical competence, stamina and confidence needed to perform convincingly and reliably. Audiences will not pay more than once to see a mediocre band and, while fans will accept occasional lapses in quality from their favourite original artist, they are less lenient towards an imitator.[9]

Checking Out the Credentials of High Flyers

Of those I encountered, the most skilled individuals command a high degree of respect and admiration, not only from their peers but from the artists they imitate as well. Far from being creatively challenged, they manage to find time to engage in original projects outside their regular work. I regularly came across musicians who had worked in successful original bands, a few even held degrees and diplomas in music or were engaged in advanced level teaching. The achievements of Wanda Ortiz of the Californian band The Iron Maidens are particularly impressive:

> Shortly after I received my music degree, I obtained an MBA (Master of Business Administration) degree from Pepperdine University. In addition to playing music, I run a business with a friend (in the technology field). It works out great because I can take off whenever I want to tour, spend time with family, or do other things for personal enrichment (I took a trip to the UK last year – it was great!). I like having a lot of options in life. (Wanda Ortiz, email, August 2007)

Like Wanda, the members of T Rextasy are equally accomplished performers. Prior to joining the band, lead singer, Danielz wrote and recorded singles which were subsequently distributed by an established label. He had a recording/songwriting deal in the early 1980s and worked on his own compositions with various high-profile artists. Danielz said his co-workers in T Rextasy are equally respected professionals, all having released original material at some point in their careers.[10] Furthermore, T Rextasy are one of a small number of tribute acts to be offered a record deal in their own right: they have released singles and albums featuring well-known material written by Marc Bolan alongside Danielz's own original compositions. The band have often performed in concert with original members of T Rex and Marc Bolan's son Rolan Bolan has joined them on stage.

The Counterfeit Stones have particularly respectable pedigrees. Before embarking on a career playing Mick Jagger, Steve Elson worked as a promoter, plugger, booker and session musician. During the 1980s he wrote and produced several hit records while later in his career, he worked with many well known artists including Status Quo, Eddie Grant, Latoya Jackson and The Baby Animals.[11] The Counterfeit's "Keith Richards". Bill Lennon is another gifted individual and a graduate of the London Guitar Institute, where he achieved the award for "best live performer of the year." Bass player Alan Mian displays a tremendous range of talents. During his career he has worked with such luminaries as Wynton Marsalis and Julian Joseph, he was musical director for the Blues Brothers stage show and if that wasn't enough, he is regularly in demand as a session player. I was even more surprised to discover that within this busy schedule, he manages to finds time to work as an instructor at the Bass Institute.[12] Involvement with external projects is common amongst high-calibre tribute artists whose ability to engage with challenging and interesting work (musical or otherwise) illustrate very clearly, Finnegan's (1999) research findings on the working lives of musicians where there is a considerable overlap between musical "worlds" and multiple creative practices.

From Familiarity to Fandom: Reasons for Paying Tribute

Regardless of their level of success or ability as original artists, musicians who decide to move into imitative entertainment are faced with a difficult choice. This dilemma is one which has troubled creatives ever since the making of music became a commercial, rather than a social activity. Wills and Cooper (1988) acknowledge that music making is a highly stressful occupation, while Martin (1995) claims the stresses are further aggravated by the problems of reconciling creative freedom with pressure to earn a living. On the one hand, paying homage might involve giving up on artistic aspirations and sacrificing a degree of freedom, but the pressure to earn money from original work can also lead to unhealthy levels of tension and frustration. Imitative performance does at least, offer the potential of a regular income however, those who make this choice intending to return to a career as an original artist, may find that their decision effectively closes off this option. Morrow, a veteran of the original and cover scene (2006: 192) explains the dilemma arguing that, "While working both the original and cover circuits is necessary, perceptions of commercial motivation can lead to career death for rock artists who are interested in being known for producing original music."

A more reliable income is only one of the motivating factors however – reasons for joining a tribute are as varied as the members themselves. Kurutz (2008: 5), in a study of the Rolling Stones tribute Sticky Fingers, expresses the popular view that, "Playing in a tribute band offers a second chance to experience stardom," but few of those I met had deliberately set out with this objective in mind. Chance encounters were occasionally cited but by far the most common reasons given, were frequent comparisons with the original artist, extreme fandom or financial imperatives.

Looking or Sounding Like the Archetype

Michael White found that regular comparisons with Robert Plant propelled him forth on the path to imitation, mainly because the similarity between his voice and Robert Plant's was having a detrimental impact on his attempts to establish himself as an original artist. He said that record companies in the mid-1970s weren't prepared to sign acts that sounded anything like Led Zeppelin because at this time, heavy rock had been supplanted by glam and punk and the screaming tenor vocal style was no longer fashionable. He also happened to bear more than a fleeting resemblance to his archetype, so, in the spirit of "if you can't beat 'em join 'em," he opted to make positive use of the likeness by paying tribute to Led Zeppelin – a wise move as it turned out – his career has lasted for over thirty years.

Paul Higginson of Stereotonics recounted a similar experience. Early in his career, he performed in a Britpop covers band but regular comments on the similarity of his voice with that of Kelly Jones, lead singer of Stereophonics, led him to opt for a career change. Initial response from agents was quite positive but none of them were willing to risk offers of work. Nevertheless, the move paid off. Within six months of forming the tribute he found that three-quarters of his bookings were for work as Stereotonics rather than his covers band. Paul's ability to portray Jones so effectively is not entirely the result of his marked likeness to the star, when not playing in Stereotonics, his well-developed acting skills enable him to devote another substantial part of his working life to portraying Liam Gallagher in the tribute band – Oasish (Figure 5.1).[13]

Jose Maldonado's decision to dedicate himself to the task of performing as Morrissey in Los Angeles based tribute Sweet and Tender Hooligans, was made after several years struggling to establish himself in an original band.

Figure 5.1 Paul Higginson (Oasish) (photograph Kevin Ryan, by permission)

The move was prompted by favourable responses to the original band's once yearly excursion into imitative entertainment at a Morrissey/The Smiths convention. Their decision to switch to homage paid off since it has enabled them to perform before enthusiastic audiences throughout the US and the UK and Maldonado was recently cast as Morrissey in a feature length film.[14] As all members of Sweet and Tender Hooligans already had good prior knowledge of the Smiths' repertoire and, since Maldonado's resemblance to Morrissey is so striking, the career shift was relatively easy for them.

For others the transition is not quite as straightforward and even though the physical resemblance is acceptable, there can be problems matching aspirational artist to repertoire. There is more to joining a tribute than throwing on a wig and grabbing a reproduction instrument. The ability to mimic the voice of the original artist for example, puts particular pressure on would-be frontmen who, charged with lead vocal, must take on board the challenge of matching their favoured artist's range. Songs are normally recorded in a particular key which may not be achievable, but as the original key plays a big part in influencing the song's identity, any variation will have a noticeable impact on the acceptability of a copy. It helps of course, if the aspirational artist is aware of these technical issues through prior knowledge of the repertoire but surprisingly, this is not always the case. Los Angeles guitarist Lenny Mann said he accepted the role of Jimmy Page in Led Zepagain knowing little about the original band's music and Nathan Morris confided that he knew nothing about the Sex Pistols prior to accepting the role of Johnny Rotter in the Sex Pistols Experience.[15] This is hard to believe as his performance style and appearance are so remarkably similar to his prototype's (see Figure 5.2).

Figure 5.2 Nathan Morris (photograph Kevin Ryan, by permission)

Taking Fandom to Extremes: the Superfans

Johnny Rotter's case is rather unusual because the majority of new recruits have plenty of knowledge – usually gained from the user-perspective of the fan community. Quite a few of those I interviewed joined or formed a tribute in order to extend the parameters of their own fandom and in some respects, this is a logical move. Musicians are often fans of the highest order and their admiration for a particular artist or band can be so all-consuming that the drift towards impersonation seems almost inevitable. Graham Sampson, "Morrissey" in British tribute The Smyths told me he and his fellow band members are all passionate Smiths fans. He felt that this shared love, enabled them to create a very sincere and authentic tribute, qualities he saw as the *sine qua non* for their discerning and erudite fan community. Sampson takes his role very seriously, likening the role of Morrissey to that of King Lear in terms of the dramaturgic challenge it evokes. This is because playing Morrissey requires a respectful and sensitive approach, where care must be exercised to avoid falling into the trap of lampooning or parody. For friendship based "superfan" bands like The Smyths, their in-depth knowledge of the original band's repertoire and performance style gives them an immediate advantage over any competitors who lack this degree of intimacy with the archetype. Following nine months of painstaking rehearsal, they were ready to unleash their homage before an audience which has occasionally included members of the original band. Where the uniform passion of The Smyths inspires them to perform, other bands are in the unfortunate position of having to battle with apathy or lack of commitment from fellow musicians who do not share their love. A member of a fledgling Thin Lizzy tribute described the problems that can arise from such a musical mismatch:

> Two members in the band aren't very big Thin Lizzy fans, and they don't want to dress up in that sort of style. This can also be a problem when it comes to practice as they can sometimes get bored of playing the songs and not want to practice. (Steve, Tizz Lizzy: interview, 12 December 2007)

A Close Encounter With Destiny

Obviously it helps it you are a fan and the transition from fandom to stardom is a logical career move for the impassioned, but the trajectory can also be the result of a totally unpredicted encounter or incident. When asked how she became a member of The Iron Maidens, lead vocalist Aja Kim told me that this was the result of informal matchmaking:

> I was referred to our bassist Wanda Ortiz by a mutual friend of ours, a very talented and well known session violinist here in LA, Dr James Sitterly, who had just recorded a string quartet tribute to Iron Maiden and knew the music quite well. I've known him for years and worked with him on numerous occasions. He was very excited about the band and thought we would be a good fit. He was right and the rest is history in the making! (Aja Kim, email, September 2004)

Countering the stereotype of tribute entertainer as shameless opportunist, Kim was already a successful musician and songwriter, having worked in a freelance capacity for major as well as independent record labels. Her motivation for joining The Iron Maidens was informed purely by curiosity and the desire for a challenge:

> I was not actually looking to do a tribute project *per se*, though I've sung plenty of covers over the years. I was intrigued by this band in particular, because it was the music of Iron Maiden being played by women. There are very few female bands out there playing such heavy and complicated music either as a tribute or as an original band and, as a woman, I loved the challenge of singing Bruce Dickinson style vocals. It's opened up a whole new world for me as a singer. (Aja Kim, email, April 2004)

Wayne Ellis of Limehouse Lizzy experienced a similar destiny moment when he and fellow band member Greg were both working in a London guitar shop. One day, on hearing Greg strumming Thin Lizzy's *Dancing in the Moonlight*, Wayne began to sing the words, impressing everyone in the shop and from here, the boys were invited to play warm up at a party where their partnership was commended. However, since there had never been a plan to make this a career, and despite being approached by an agent, Ellis admitted to being half appalled and half intrigued by the idea of performing someone else's work for a living. The band are now one of the most popular on the scene, regularly selling out at venues up and down the UK and abroad.[16]

Making the Most of the Faustian Bargain

In some instances, the decision to work in a tribute band is a purely pragmatic one – fuelled by the desire to play live before an enthusiastic audience and the prospect of a half decent income. Hardly surprising when taking into account the financial realities experienced by the average musician: a recent study (Riley and Laing 2006) revealed that half of the jazz musicians in the UK earn under £10,000 a year. Few would fail to empathize with drummer Dave, aka Paul Crook of The Sex Pistols Experience, whose epiphany moment came after a disastrous excursion to Sheffield with an original band.

> My turning point came one night after having travelled three hours to get to play a gig, this was back in around 1990, a time before computers and the Internet when it was all done over the phone and you couldn't find out where the best places to play were unless you lived there. We arrived at the gig, set up and waited for the crowd to arrive – as they had done in our local region. (Dave, interview, November 2007)

In spite of their valiant efforts to promote the gig by sending posters and flyers in advance, when the band finally arrived, they discovered that nobody had taken the trouble to display them. In the spirit of show business – the band played on:

> So we do the gig, to no more than eight people, four of whom we'd taken along with us. Having paid out for the cost of making and copying posters and flyers that went unused, the travel expenses plus all the effort – for nothing, no gain whatsoever, then to add insult to injury – having to shell out £50 (for in-house PA hire)for the "pleasure" of it, I came to the conclusion that if I'm going to sacrifice my weekends by not seeing my girlfriend or my mates like normal people do, I might just as well give up this idea of playing original music, banging my head against the wall and do a load of popular cover versions, play to a healthy crowd, have a great time AND get paid for doing it. (Dave, interview, November 2007)

Dave's views resonate with those of Ian Watts, "Paul McCartney" in The Beatalls, who felt that although his early career as an original musician had enabled him to tour and perform his own music, playing Paul McCartney provided a challenge with a far greater financial reward. He can now afford to spend time recording original music with expensive equipment in his own recording studio – a luxury he would not have been able to enjoy in his days as a struggling original artist.

Choosing the Right Artist

A lot depends on choosing the right artist as the wrong choice will have major implications regarding future income and success.[17] While critics may be in the position to disparage popular taste, caution must be exercised in resurrecting the work of less popular artists or unfashionable genres. The most highly paid tributes are those which imitate the work of artists who enjoyed international acclaim during their heyday. Their success provides a large instant fan base whereas the reverse is true in the case of more obscure artists. However, the fact that the most popular artists already have plenty of tributes makes it difficult for the up-and-coming to find a niche in an already crowded field, and the competition is exacerbated by fans' tendency to develop an allegiance to their favourite tribute, leaving minimal room for newcomers.

The decision regarding who to pay tribute to can have quite unexpected and sometimes, undesirable repercussions. A downturn in the fortunes of the original band for example, may have a sudden, disastrous impact. Following the demise of British band The Darkness, their imitators experienced a parallel reversal in demand for their services but all is not necessarily lost! One management company Svengali recommends expedience: "a lot of them have invested in good quality equipment, a van, that sort of stuff – if you're running it properly as a business, you have to keep it going" (Petridis 2007) . He suggests that The Darkness doubles might just as well turn their hands to paying homage to another, more popular band. In fact any change in the original artist's fortunes will have an impact on the career of their tribute. For instance, in response to the ups and downs of Robbie Williams' career some of his tributes have had to take stock and diversify. According to Patrick Haveron, who manages over 200 acts, it is important to stay ahead of the game. One of his artists, Gavin Munn, recently switched from being Robbie to playing Billie Joe Armstrong in the tribute band Green Dayz. He also cited the case of a Geri Halliwell look-alike who turned her hand to playing Shakira for a while before metamorphosing yet again – this time into Pink![18] Playing out the situation in reverse, the meteoric rise of reformed Take That has led to a potential oversupply of tributes, including Fake That, Take That 2, Take This, Take 2 That, Re-Take That and Back 4 Good.

The Devil is in the Detail – Technical Issues

Once artist and repertoire are established, a great deal of effort needs to be put into providing the level of accuracy expected by fans. In a competitive, dog-eat-dog world, even for the successful, the threat of up-and-coming competition looms. Anyone wanting to stay at the top of their game needs to pay very careful attention to the smallest details to keep their audience happy. According to Greg Blackman, guitarist in US Led Zeppelin tribute Winds of Thor, many factors are involved in achieving the correct musical accuracy:

> Generally speaking, the band members need to be EXTREMELY detail oriented. There are tons of little nuances in Zeppelin songs that make these songs sound the way they do. Often time they are things that are barely noticeable, like a ghost note on the drums or a grace note on the guitar. If those things are absent, the songs just won't sound right and the audience will know it's off but probably won't be able to pin-point why. (Greg Blackman, interview, September 2008)

He goes on to describe the importance of matching the style of the original musician, offering the example of Zeppelin drummer John Bonham:

> Bonham was a master of the single pedal bass drum. Any drummer using a double bass to play these songs will never match the groove and feel of these songs. Zeppelin was known for long improvisational jams. A good Zeppelin tribute will be able to go off and jam in the middle of a song doing whatever and still sound like Zeppelin. (Greg Blackman, interview, September 2008)

Then there are the technical issues surrounding accurate sound reproduction and lighting which can be equally taxing, as the Bootleg Beatles (Figure 5.3) explain.

Figure 5.3 The Bootleg Beatles (Raj Patel, by permission)

> It's all about trying to get the right balance of instruments (the band use authentic guitars through VOX amps which usually produces the genuine Beatle sound) and vocals. The vocal impersonation is imperative, but also the echos/reverbs that are used on the vocals are vital ... e.g. the delay on Lennon's voice in a song like *A day in the life*. We also use certain Beatle sound effects (applause in "with a little help" or "jet engine" in *Back in USSR*). These need to be triggered at the correct times. (Bootleg Beatles, email, March 2009).

With a view to achieving perfection, another group resorted to employing the services of their archetype's technicians. Not only do The Australian Pink Floyd use identical equipment to that used by The Floyd on tour, they also recruited the original band's light and sound crew members to get the details right (Muendel 2008).This attention to detail can become all-consuming, driving some musicians to unimaginable extremes When asked how he prepared for his role in The Beatles tribute The Beatalls, musician Ian Watts said:

> I play Paul McCartney so I sing all his parts, including the correct harmony if three are going at once. I play the bass line and I have had to convert from being a natural right handed player to being a left handed player! I have to speak like him, walk, move and look like him as much as possible and react to situations in the way I believe he would. The art is to play the music as closely as possible listening in great detail to the drum rolls, instrument notes, vocal lines, accents, etc. Mad I know but its all part of the full tribute. (Ian Watts, interview, July 2004)

Looking the Part

Musicianship skills alone will not always attract an audience. The fact that audiences enjoy the pleasure of looking means artists have to pay careful attention to their appearance, making the most of their natural attributes, minimizing discrepancies, while learning how to simulate a genre's identity codes. If there are existing physical similarities this can be relatively straightforward, but if there is a mismatch, acting skills and body modification can be used as an aid to representation – the closer the match, the higher the rewards. Wayne Ellis told me that early in their career Limehouse Lizzy attracted a particularly macho, biker audience of male Thin Lizzy fans. Recognizing the importance of attracting a wider fan base, he encouraged fellow band members to work out in order to improve their physique. They also upgraded their wardrobes to include more glamorous stage outfits such as leather trousers and body-hugging, Lycra T-shirts (Figure 5.4).

These endeavours to improve upon natural attributes, remind us of the fabricated nature of stardom and the work required to achieve it.

> The work of fashioning the star out of the raw material of the person, varies in the degree to which it respects what artists sometimes refer to as the inherent qualities of the material; make up, coiffure, clothing, dieting and body-building can all make more or less of the body features they start with, and personality is no less malleable, skills no less learnable. (Dyer 2004: 5)

Ellis is a gifted performer who oozes charm and confidence both on and off stage: he has such tremendous presence that one suspects the task of inhabiting the star identity is relatively easy for him. The resemblance to his archetype Phil Lynott is achieved primarily through the medium of charisma and self-possession and it is these qualities, rather than perfectly matched physical similarities, which enable him to offer such a credible likeness. The conviction he brings to his performance recalls Goffman's (1959: 28) observation

Figure 5.4 Limehouse Lizzy (photograph Wayne Ellis, by permission)

that, if the performer "can be fully taken in by his own act; he can be sincerely convinced that the impression of reality which he stages is the real reality." This confidence, effectively, gives permission to the audience to set aside their disbelief to collude with the illusion being presented.

Artists who avoid direct mimicking of looks or mannerisms prefer instead, to be authentic to their own character, operating more as a channel for the original artist's personality and musicianship. For these individuals, there is no need to act since they can rely on a combination of intuition and instinct. T. Rextasy frontman Danielz describes his approach:

> I don't agree with wearing wigs or playing to backing discs. I have never studied Marc's moves – it's always been in me ... I don't get into character and we are all the same on-stage as off stage. Again, we are lucky enough to have got away with being practically 50% original to ourselves, even though we are still a tribute to Marc Bolan. In concert I lengthen songs, I shorten them, I say things that Marc would never have said on stage – mainly because I still retain my own personality. (Danielz, email, May 2007)

Danielz does have the natural advantage of looking strikingly similar to Marc Bolan and this undoubtedly helps him to step so readily into his position as frontman (see Figure 5.5).

Figure 5.5 Danielz (photograph Danielz, by permission)

In Lee Sullivan of Roxy Magic's case, physical dissimilarity to his archetype, saxophonist Andy Mackay, made the onstage transition more challenging. In order to bring credibility to his role, a combination of in-depth study and improvisation was necessary.

> I was previously in a short-lived Roxy Music tribute called Foxy Music and videotaped the handful of performances we gave. I studied what I was doing carefully and refined my stage moves according to what I thought did not work; for example I tried a duck-walk during a particular solo. Being more hefty than Mackay this was not terribly attractive, though it did mutate into a "walkabout" – something Mackay never did – amongst the audience where stage height permitted. I suppose that this also shows that we do allow our "real" selves to peep through. (Lee Sullivan, email May 2007)

Sullivan's challenge is relatively straightforward though, when compared to that faced by Paul Higginson, who alternates between two characters in the tribute bands Stereotonics and Oasish. This means recreating the vocal and performance styles of two highly distinctive and decidedly dissimilar frontmen, sometimes at the same gig. When asked what preparation was necessary, he said it was quite difficult getting the "acting" just right on stage. More so for Kelly Jones than Liam Gallagher.

> Everyone knows that when Liam sings, he leans to one side, puts his arms behind his back and tilts his head back to sing into the mic. With Kelly Jones however, it's a much more demanding presence in terms of movement. There is a lot of foot stomping and mannerisms that have had to be perfected. Again, endless hours of watching live footage of both bands has helped no end in this. It's almost a kind of research project when a new DVD comes out to see if they are doing anything different (Paul Higginson, email, May 2007).

The problems of creating a credible simulation, are further magnified within a band where all of the musicians are playing in character. Sex Pistol's Experience drummer Dave recounted the problem of finding the right combination of looks and talent. He explained that though looks were taken into account when auditioning, and three of his band members do bear more than a passing resemblance to the artists they imitate, their bass player is nothing like The Sex Pistol's party animal and well-built ladies' man, Steve Jones.

> In a full tribute band, to get all four or five in a group spot-on is near impossible and well done if you manage it. But we have a tea-drinking, eight stone skinny bloke, who gets very little attention other than for his playing abilities. People in the audience do look for cracks in a tribute, "Oh that's not right, this isn't right, he's got the wrong colour shirt" or whatever. So we get, "Oh you three are spot-on, but not sure about him.!?." It does get tiring and tedious: to get "everything" right is tough, especially when it comes to the personal attributes of individual players within the group when nothing can be done about it. (Dave, email, June 2008)

The job of recreating the musical career and characters of The Sex Pistols is relatively easy though, when compared to the task of simulating the lengthy and enduring career of The Rolling Stones. Steve Elson, said The Counterfeit Stones must use up to 24 different guitars, numerous costume changes and even changes in personnel in their recreation of the iconic band's working life. This means that core band members Nick Dagger, Keef Rickard, Bill Hymen and Charlie Mott must be accompanied at different points in the show by either Bryon Jones, Mick Taylor-Made or Ronnie B Goode. This spectacular level of attention to detail is beyond the capability of the majority of tributes but it does illustrate differences in the degree of difficulty musicians face. For most, it will be enough if only key band members match the audience's expectations and the pressure to look right will normally fall most heavily upon the lead singers and lead guitarists. Bass player Wanda Ortiz describes these issues in relation to her own band.

> As far as pressure goes, it depends on the tribute band and on the individual. In Iron Maiden, although every member is important, people have a tendency to notice the singer (Bruce Dickinson) and bass player (Steve Harris) more. In Rush, people think of the drummer and bass player (who also sings). In Mötley Crüe, it seems like people think of mostly the drummer Tommy Lee. So ... if you're in that spot, it's true that people might notice you more than other members of the band but I think all you can do is do your best and not worry about. (Wanda Ortiz, email, August 2007)

In The Counterfeit Stones' case, Steve Elson said that fans have a tendency to make a beeline for either himself (as lead singer Mick Jagger) or whoever is playing Keith Richards. While drummers can usually hide at the back of the stage, the greater visibility of the key protaganists places particular demands on their physical and mental state.

Maintaining Physical and Mental Fitness

The intense pressure on lead singers means that they can't afford to have an 'off' day. The band's livelihood is dependent on reliability and non-stop touring, moreover, fans and promoters can be unforgiving. Wayne Ellis said he has to be careful to maintain his vocal capacity and overall physical fitness in order to perform on such a regular basis. Steve Elson too. strives to maintain his fitness with a regular exercise regime – something of a necessity when charged with the role of hyperactive athlete Mick Jagger. It is helpful if physical fitness is linked to a positive mental outlook. This is because success depends on the maintenance of good interpersonal relationships within the group. The tensions between famous band members are well-documented but at least they could face the prospect of time away from one another between tours and the recording studio. A balanced temperament helps, as does an uncomplicated personal life, as Dave of the Sex Pistol's Experience explains.

> There are some important other factors to take into consideration which are often overlooked by bands who can make do with the bloke up the road who's got a guitar. This may be fine for pub bands, cover bands, or semi pro groups – we being a professional touring band, need someone who can commit to being away from home days, or sometimes weeks,

> at a time. Someone who doesn't have "personal issues" and we feel we can all get along with, is not out just for the free booze and good times, but a serious minded musician focused on the job, no drug problems, no criminal record (as you can't get work visas) easy to get on with, has an understanding partner. (Dave, email, June 2008)

Dave's observations show that musical ability by itself, is not necessarily enough. Successful musicians, like other professionals in the modern workplace working in teams, need to be equipped with a whole range of personal and social skills. These findings are carefully airbrushed out of the discourses of popular music, which focus instead on narratives of virtuosity and individual creativity.

Promoting the Brand

Once the repertoire has been mastered – a competent (and hopefully co-operative) band assembled, anyone wishing to make an impact on the scene must establish their identity there. Like other modern enterprises charged with the problem of marketing a product, tribute acts must invest some money in the creation of a recognizable corporate image if they are to keep abreast of the competition. Negus (2001: 72) writes that branding in popular music, allows the, "unique quality of an act [to] become instantly recognisable and condensed into a specific image which could become a trademark". These trademarks, many of which are imbued with meaning and historical significance, are viewed by fans as hallmarks of authenticity and to a great extent, the look of music can be more memorable than the music itself. Negus (2001: 66) elaborates this point, citing the research findings of a record label executive who played a word association game where people were asked to choose a genre and then respond with the first thing that came to mind. It seems that we see what we hear and the public identify most strongly with music's images as a staggering 99 per cent of respondents gave an answer which referred to a visual association.

Logos, as the pictorial counterpart of a brand, enable audiences to identify with the original band's identity. These "miniature visual narratives" (Danesi 2006) can tap into the their emotional and sensory connection with the brand, reassuring them that the tribute, like the logo is "the real thing." Authentication is further reinforced on promotional material and web pages through careful reference to the colours and fonts used by the archetype. For example, as most Thin Lizzy tributes make use of a trademark mirrored onstage backdrop and the band's instantly recognizable angular logo, any newcomers will need to adhere to the house style (Figure 5.6) if they wish to claim a share of the market.

Figure 5.6 (a) Tizz Lizzy and (b) Twin Lizzy Logos (Steve Edgar, by permission, and www.myspace.com/twinlizzyofficial)

Naming is another major aspect of brand identity. Ironically, in a world defined by mimicry, care must be taken to avoid the duplication of any existing band names. There must though, be some connection to the original act. Tributes will sometimes deliberately draw attention to their appropriation by making cheekily open references to their theft or simulation of the prototype's identity, as do Fake That, The Bootleg Beatles, The Counterfeit Stones and The Clone Roses. For others such as The Australian Doors, The Japanese Beatles and The Benwell Floyd, staking a claim on a geographical area allows them to assume an imagined audience and national or regional affiliations. Then there are names which speak directly to the aficionado through reference to an obscure aspect of the original band's history. Using the name Hollywood Rose, for instance, ensures that only the more knowledgeable Guns and Roses fans are addressed, thereby appealing to the popular music connoisseurship identified by Straw (1997).[19]

Finding Work and Maintaining Professional Standards

With repertoire and image perfected, work must be found. Popular mythology suggests that musicians who enter this field of work do so to make easy money but, at any given time, several tributes to the same band will be in search of work. Only a limited number can expect to obtain regular bookings at any of the larger venues and the rest will find it hard to survive on the modest remuneration from working the smaller clubs and pubs. Acts like Bjorn Again are able to fill major arenas but the newly established bands wishing to establish a reputation need initially to work their way up. For a number of reasons, this can take some time – as Raj Patel, manager of internationally successful tribute band The Bootleg Beatles explains:

> The problem that tribute bands face is that a lot of the larger venues will not consider taking many of the lesser known acts and will often take on just the one tribute to a certain band: they will not book more than one Beatles, one Queen band, etc. However, there are plenty of small theatres around and as their overheads tend to be quite small, they will be more willing to consider your act. (Raj Patel 2001)

In the UK, the industry also experiences seasonal fluctuations and it is harder to tempt an audience to spend an evening in the theatre during the summer months when there is competition from music festivals. For this reason, the best months of go on tour are February through to April. This period also helps newcomers to overcome competition generated by big name tributes in the weeks leading to Christmas.

The importance of behaving in a professional manner cannot be overlooked. Strong interpersonal communication skills are valued in any career but in one where self-promotion is so vital, they are essential. When carrying out my research, I noticed that successful bands, mindful of the importance of public relations, were quick to respond to requests for information. Quite a few of my interviewees were polite, charming and persuasive and no doubt the same skills are put to use in securing work and maintaining good communication with the audience. Martyn of So '80s, spoke of the need for a thoroughly professional approach:

> We never sit back and think "we've done all the hard work, now let's wait for the phone to ring." Maintaining the highest standards on and off stage keep the job enjoyable and the diary busy. It's a business, not a weekend hobby. You can only be as good as your best, not only on stage but off stage with clients. Never under-estimate the importance of how you market yourself. (Martyn, email June 2009)

Complacency is a mindset to be avoided at all costs – the competitive nature of the live industry continually fuels rivalry – with individual bands fighting it out to maintain a position at the top of their game – in the words of one veteran.

> The competition is fierce – it's a dog eat dog world out there. You have to show you are the best. When one of our guitarists left we replaced him by taking on a member of one of our rival bands. It might sound arrogant but we know we can do this because we are the best Thin Lizzy tribute. (Wayne Ellis, Limehouse Lizzy, interview, May 2007)

In extreme cases, the rivalry can lead to the employment of underhand guerrilla tactics the more scurrilous methods can involve ripping down posters, cancelling gigs and disrupting social networking sites. Jurgen of The Smiths Indeed, recounted his band's experience of the latter skulduggery: "We have had our MySpace account cancelled 5 times in 2 years (after building up a sizeable following of thousands of fans each time)" (Jurgen, email, October 2008). Although he told me that he didn't like to think this had been carried out by a competitor, he had noticed that a rival Smiths' tribute always seemed to be playing in London the night before The Smiths Indeed were due to perform there.

Taking Care of Business

As if there wasn't enough to do already. In addition to warding off the competition, running a band requires a great deal of administration. There is simply so much work. If they have one, the majority of this activity will be carried out by the band's manager, but in the case of self-managing outfits, business duties must be added to the demands of performance and travel. Steve Elson of The Counterfeit Stones combines administrative duties and site meetings with IT and accounting jobs.

> I would spend the Monday going through the accounts and receipts for the preceding week. These can be any thing from "On the road" expenses like fuel, hotels, etc. to the office and production bills. There's often a number of queries to deal with like somebody's hotel room was infested with ants or the amp repair wasn't satisfactory. Then there's the email traffic. This can be made up of gig enquiries, theatre publicity requests, technical questions for forthcoming shows, etc. On other days in the week I often have to go to site and production meetings. A lot of private shows are held in rich people's houses and I usually have to go along and meet the party planner to work out what equipment we need and how it's going to be loaded in, set up and loaded out. On a show of our size you cannot leave this to

> chance and I've avoided an awful lot of hassle by seeing the premises and discussing the logistics well in advance. (Steve Elson, interview, September 2007)

The planning of corporate events requires particularly strong project planning and time management skills.

> Corporate shows are complicated in other ways. We're often part of a bigger bill and timing for these events is crucial and so every aspect of equipment setup and stage space allocation has to be discussed so that The Counterfeit Stones don't get into a war with Jo Brand's manager about who's nicking the best stage real estate. A lot of these shows are held in premises that weren't designed for live bands but the client craves originality and so we've ended up doing shows in the Natural History Museum, Tower Bridge, The London Dungeon and at the top of a mountain in St Moritz. Without lots of meetings and planning these events would go horribly wrong. (Steve Elson, interview, September 2007)

In his working week Elson demonstrates that he is a competent communicator and leader who knows how to use networking to good effect, again illustrating the ubiquity of his skills and their importance in the day-to-day management of the band.

> My other tasks include briefing the rest of the band and crew on the arrangements for the forthcoming shows. There are ten in our party and all want thorough details. I also have to monitor travel conditions so that I can advise alternative routes and parking places. In and around this I have to hussle for gigs, design posters, leaflets and brochures, edit video, and do interviews, press releases, etc. (Steve Elson, interview, May 2007)

Limehouse Lizzy, another of the minority of UK tributes who make a full-time living from their craft, is run by Wayne Ellis who takes responsibility for accounts, bookings, merchandising and public relations. These self-managing bands have certain advantages in that they have greater freedom to decide when and where to work, who to employ and how to market themselves. Since they are the main beneficiaries of their efforts, they have everything to gain by operating proactively. Ellis maintains a clear "vision" which includes making the band an attractive place to be (by offering members financial security), only playing good-quality venues which yield a reasonable ticket price, and keeping demand high by limiting appearances at any given venue to once in every 18 months. He also ensures that gigs are around fifty miles apart to avoid over-saturation and audience complacency.

Rock and pop histories frequently overlook the sheer volume of work involved in touring. In fact, a great deal of practical work must be undertaken to maintain the coherence of the illusory world represented onstage. Iron Maidens' Jenny Warren's account of essential tasks illustrates some of the complexities involved.

> A dedicated person needs to be able to run around, collect waiver forms, get them signed, turn them in, get photo clearance passes/ all access crew passes/parking validation stickers, coordinate with the sound guy, check policies and procedures on merchandise set up, review all sound cues with the sound guy, get water to the band, co-ordinate the dressing room facilities, brief the camera/video photographer, set up the dinner details etc. (Jenny Warren, 'Combatting the Big Gig Blues', *Tribute City*, June 2001)

Although this unglamorous work is essential to the production, it is carried out backstage where it is concealed from the audience. In the chaotic parallel world behind the scenes, planning and attention to detail ensures that the illusion remains untarnished. In a rundown of a typical day, The Bootleg Beatles offer some insight into the practicalities of stage management.

> The load in each day usually starts at about 10 o'clock. All the gear is positioned and the lights flown before the PA stacks are built and the back-line positioned. The crews (sound, light and backline) work at assembly and preparation for sound check at 4 p.m. when the band and orchestra arrive. This takes quite a while on day one but as the tour progresses so it reduces in time. Once the sound check is over it's time for catering, eating and then preparing for the show. Normally the show runs for two and a half hours including interval. The break down of equipment starts the moment the last chords of "Let it Be" are ringing in the hall. Within two hours both band and crew are on buses and on the road to the next venue. (The Bootleg Beatles, email July 2008)

Sources of Tension and Life on the Road

With good practical support and a positive attitude, the rigours of touring are minimized. For successful bands with a heavy duty touring schedule, this helps to reduce the tensions which inevitably build up when on the road. In the record industry, the purpose of the tour is to help break the career of fledgling bands and it is an important tool for establishing and nurturing a fan base but for tribute acts, it constitutes the entire working life. If the competition is to be kept at bay and fans satisfied, successful tribute musicians can expect to spend a good deal of time away from friends and family, although surprisingly little of this time will be spent on playing music. Whole Lotta Led estimated that performance only amounts to 20 per cent of the average day in what looks like a punishing lifestyle:

> The travelling is constant – we do over a hundred shows a year. Our manager Rick drives and most days we travel up and down the motorway in a van, staying in Premier Lodge Inns. There is no social life outside the band and a lot of our time is spent checking equipment, making sound checks and sitting around to kill time when we are waiting to get on stage. (Whole Lotta Led, interview, November 2007)

From Wanda Ortiz's point of view, travelling is problematic as it can lead to boredom and an unhealthy lifestyle. She describes some of the difficulties and her band's strategies for dealing with them.

> It's hard to stay in shape when on the road – seems like all there is to eat is fast food. With this in mind, we try to plan ahead and bring healthy snacks and water. Working out can be a challenge because it's hard to do when you're driving or you're on a tight schedule so we just roll with the punches. If I have a couple hours off in a new city, I like to take long walks and check out the scenery. I know our singer likes to do sit ups – everyone just kind of figures out their own routine as they go along. (Wanda Ortiz, email, August 2007)

Debunking the myth of the rock musician as a freewheeling aesthete, band schedules can seem more exhausting than those of high-flying executives. Chronicling an average day, Jaymz of Beatallica said, "We are probably up till about 2 a.m., then up again between 8–10 a.m. ... typically, sleep isn't plentiful, so we try to zonk out as we go." Various methods are used to while away the time in less than luxurious transport.

> Our travel van in the US is simply your average large van with seats, room for gear, and semi-comfortable. We take along a DVD player for something to do, but I'm really into crossword puzzles so I'm using my head/brain instead of sitting for hours on end. In Europe, our sprinter is cool, plenty of room. We do try to keep things clean and do "housework" as needed. (Jaymz, email, August 2007)

Despite the physical limitations and sleep deprivation, Jaymz felt on balance, that the experience of touring was enjoyable. However, like a lot of his fellows, he spoke of the importance of trying to maintain some distance from colleagues.

> Well, it can be fun – it should be fun – you are with friends and making music, meeting new folks, seeing new places, but it can be a looooonnnnggg [*sic*] day. Getting up early, travelling every day, not sleeping much, not eating the best at times. Friends are friends but we do like to be away from each other for periods at a time to keep our relationship fresh, the tunes as well ... even if we are home, we prefer to spend ample amount of time apart. (Jaymz, email, August 2007)

Roxy Magic sax player Lee Sullivan was equally keen to warn of the dangers of spending too much time together.

> Don't spend social time with band members – familiarity breeds contempt – just have a great time when the band gets together! Make sure one has resources for good PA systems and engineers and roadies where possible. (Lee Sullivan, interview May 2007)

Playing the same music on a regular basis is another source of frustration. This can lead musicians to quit the tribute scene (Steve Elson said guitarists in The Counterfeit Stones remained with the band for an average of four years) and for those who stay, different strategies must be employed to cope with the problem. Several musicians admitted to tinkering with the arrangements as a means of creating a challenge. Whole Lotta Led confided that although they never tired of playing classic Led Zeppelin, it was good to improvise a little within solos. For a few fortunate individuals, major creative opportunities are presented in-house. Danielz told me that being a member of T-Rextasy, has presented him with a unique challenge, something which has enabled him to use his expert knowledge of T-Rex to record and release original tracks.

> We are slightly lucky and different to most tribute bands. On our albums (of which we have 3 on CD, 7" release, CD single release, and 12" release), we have original songs. I have also adapted unreleased Marc Bolan tracks and re-recorded them with T-Rextasy and made them into T-Rextasy songs and we have those tracks on the albums too. The record companies also released a video and CD single called *Baby Factory* which was a self-penned number and released in the UK and Japan (which enabled us to tour Japan twice in the 15 years the band have been together). Also contained on two of our albums are four original songs written by me in the style of Bolan. (Danielz, email, May 2007)

Payback Time – Reaping the Rewards

Taking into account the challenges and insecurities of a career in the live sector and bearing in mind that there is an oversupply of musicians seeking employment, the rewards for a successful tribute are significantly higher than those of the average cover or unsigned original band. Local cover groups in the UK may charge as little as £150 for a gig and original bands operating on a "pay for play" basis may also fail to make a profit. A successful British tribute act on the other hand, can command between £900-£2,000 per night, and for those who make it into the premier league, the earnings are potentially much higher. Alive Network advertises The Bootleg Beatles for hire from £10,800 per booking and Bjorn Again have been so successful that as of 2007, at any given time, five versions of the act were simultaneously on tour in different parts of the world.

Despite the frustrations and compromises involved, working in a tribute band seems to provide musicians with many positive benefits over and above any financial security they offer. Rewards include, the chance to perform on a regular basis, to travel and to enjoy a degree of respect and admiration from fans, peers and sometimes the original artists. The job also creates opportunities for autonomy and self-direction which help to counterbalance the down side of working in the creative sector. Finally, there are many social benefits. Musicians working in tribute and cover groups may not be living the rock and roll high life but in an epoch characterized by alienation and insecurity, "banding" provides musicians with friendship, mutual support and the fellowship of the wider creative community.

6 The Value of Paying Tribute: Critical Responses

Tribute acts are generally viewed negatively and despite their relative longevity on the popular music scene, they remain stubbornly poised beyond the parameters of respectability. Hardly a marginal cultural form nowadays, the most well-known are a regular feature at high-profile events and venues: Bjorn Again for example, have played the Reading and Glastonbury Festivals in the UK, the State Theatre in Sydney and Irving Plaza in New York. However, in spite of achieving significance, incorporation into the music mainstream even, the activities of tributes are rarely covered with any gravity by the official music press. When they are represented in the media they are usually portrayed as tragically humorous, pathetic or decidedly lowbrow.[1] This matches Shuker's observations that those engaged in unoriginal performance are automatically placed at the lower end of a status hierarchy, a pecking order ranging from:

> those starting out, largely reliant on "covers," to session musicians, to performers who attempt, with varying levels of critical and commercial success, to make a living from music. This last group has its own differentiations, with notions of "journeymen" players, and hierarchies of "artists" and stars often likened to some sort of sports league table: a minor or major league band; first and second division performers, stars and "megastars." (Shuker, 2002: 112)

Regardless of the lack of any consistent criteria for judgement, the hierarchy is endorsed by critics, fans and even the musicians themselves. Why is it that nobody takes their achievements seriously, and must parodic entertainers be consigned to a critical wasteland where the doors to The Rock and Roll Hall of Fame remain permanently locked? This chapter attempts to understand the lack of recognition by investigating key discourses underpinning the attribution of value to music and more specifically, the value placed on unoriginal music and performance. Definitions of authenticity and originality will be placed within differing historical and cultural contexts in order to explore the inconsistent application of primary terms to mediate the reception of imitative music practices. In addition to the perspectives of critics the thoughts of fans, peers and the musicians themselves will be considered in order to offer a more informed understanding of conflicting viewpoints.

Philosophical Debates

The practice of imitation is as good starting point as any because an aversion to copying seems to be at the heart of the majority of critiques. Opinions on the value of replication are clearly divided with the vast majority condemning the practice. Journalist Nick Parker's (1996) observations are typical. Starting with the age old adage that, "Imitation is the sincerest form of flattery," he writes, "In the world of popular music, it is also the surest way of making up for a lack of personal creativity." Banal jibes like this pervade the reception of tributes but it is hard to see how arguments regarding the absolute authority of an original text can be sustained in an industry where imitation is so all pervasive. Nevertheless, the thoughts of anti-imitationists rule. Why then, are critics so determined to promote the idea that copying is a bad thing and are there any alternative viewpoints?

When we place the matter into a broader historical context, arguments against copying have a lengthy pedigree going back to the earliest civilizations, where philosophers wrestled with the pros and cons. In Ancient Greece, for example, both Plato and Aristotle tried to assess the worth of representation, with Plato arguing firmly against the practice. His preoccupation with eternal forms led him to the opinion that the natural world was at best an illusion and as a consequence, he believed imitative artworks could never reproduce the true essence or value of their subject.[2]

> Must we not infer that all these poetical individuals, beginning with Homer, are only imitators; they copy images of virtue and the like, but the truth they never reach? The poet is like a painter who, as we have already observed, will make a likeness of a cobbler though he understands nothing of cobbling; and his picture is good enough for those who know no more than he does, and judge only by colours and figures. (Plato 600e, Book X in Ferrari 2000)

Where Plato eschewed copying Aristotle recognized the allure of mimesis, concluding that it is natural for humans to take delight in imitation:

> it is an instinct of human beings from childhood to engage in imitation (indeed, this distinguishes them from other animals: man is the most imitative of all, and it is through imitation that he develops his earliest understanding); and it is equally natural that everyone enjoys imitative objects. (Aristotle, *Poetics* 1448b in Barnes 1999)

Double Trouble

In many respects Aristotle's thoughts capture the fascination evoked by a faithful impersonation – the close physical likeness and replication of body language, performance style, voice and virtuosity is strangely compelling. Psychoanalyst Otto Rank (1971: 49) noted a universal fascination following an encounter with a mirror image: consider for example, the delight and curiosity babies display when they see themselves for the first time or the magnetism of the personal photograph for those unfamiliar with the medium. Then there are the strange human doubles which historically elicit a wide range of responses, from positive connotations of immortality in the ancient world, to the more malign associations connected to doppelgangers. Doppelgangers, creatures who replicate another's identity, first appeared in eighteenth-century literature.[3] Their presence soon became overloaded with sinister meanings, notably in the shape of a "spectral presentiment of disaster" (Schwartz 1996: 84). The poet John Donne is said to have seen his wife's double shortly before their child was stillborn while Shelley claimed he saw a doppelganger prior to his untimely death and American president Abraham Lincoln had a similar rendezvous with his double immediately before being assassinated.

To complicate matters further, embedded within doppelganger mythology is the notion of an intra-psychic split so that, as Rogers (1970: 12) writes: "The double is of course some sort of antithetical self, usually a guardian angel or tempting devil." When they do appear, doubles possibly represent sides of ourselves we would wish to conceal but they are especially feared for their sinister potential to supplant their archetype. This theme is used to create dramatic tension by Fyodor Dostoyevsky in his hallucinatory tale, *The Double*, where a man is haunted by a look-alike, who eventually usurps his position with friends and colleagues. Edgar Allan Poe also uses the double motif in the short story *William Wilson*, where the protagonist's jealousy of his double, leads him to commit murder. Doppelganger myths only add an element of mystery to a confrontation with what looks like a mirror image of another human being but at a more fundamental level, by suggesting that replication is possible, the double threatens our deep-seated belief in the unique qualities of the individual. In the identity-obsessed culture of popular music, this creates something of a dilemma – if someone else can walk, talk, play guitar and sing like John Lennon – what does this say about his standing as a gifted artist with unique and irreplaceable ability? By showing that it is possible for someone else to perform the repertoire so accurately, the musical doubles of tribute bands have the power to dismantle the mythical status of the music industry's virtuosos.

For fans, the experience of seeing and hearing the musical equivalent of the ghostly double is mesmerizing: a precisely detailed copy of an existing artist has the power to trick them into believing the performer and the performance. They are certainly preoccupied with the subject of similarities if comments posted on band websites are anything to go on. Hardly a page goes by, without a remark about similarities to original artists. Credible likenesses receive favourable comments, whereas inaccurate ones invariably attract negative feedback. Fan comments posted on a YouTube video of The Bootleg Beatles, for example, show an obsessive preoccupation with the accuracy of the band's rendition of the *Taxman* guitar solo. The importance attached to faithful reproduction of the minutiae of performance, focuses on anxieties expressed about Bootleg Paul's right-handed bass playing on *She Loves You.*[4] Although only a minor detail, for some fans, the discrepancy is intolerable. In a similar vein fans of Thin Lizzy, keen to establish a resemblance between tribute frontman Wayne Ellis and the late Phil Lynott, marvel at what they perceive to be a close physical and vocal similarity to the deceased singer (Figure 6.1).

Figure 6.1 Wayne Ellis (photograph Wayne Ellis, by permission)

Despite the importance fans attach to imitation of identity, critics generally refuse to engage with the debates on visual fidelity, either because they see this as irrelevant or following Plato, on the grounds that a copy must be inherently inferior. They may be uncomfortable with the embodiment of identity but this is more a matter of taste and fails to explain their point-blank refusal to acknowledge the degree of skill involved in copying. The ability to perform a character requires a level of application and aptitude and not everyone is capable of offering a credible likeness but critical commentary on the matter tends to be rather unbalanced. Witness the outraged commentator who, after an excursion to a local bar where he happened upon a tribute act, directed the following diatribe towards the band:

> While I understand that you all want to be the people you're impersonating, you're not actually them, you're mostly second-rate chicken-in-the basket cabaret performers ... you're not really rock stars, so stop acting like you are ... In my opinion tribute bands are a bigger threat to proper live music than karaoke or mobile discos ever were, and they should all be put on a cruise ship, towed into the middle of the Atlantic and sunk. (Comment posted on Lemonrock live music forum, 11 September 2006)

Some may sympathize with his rant, particularly if they have spent their hard-earned cash on an evening out, only to be confronted by a group of barely competent imposters; nevertheless, complaints like these should still be challenged. Many tribute artists are excellent musicians and may even play to a higher standard than their archetypes, several of whom have give the seal of approval to their parodic brethren. Oasis invited The Bootleg Beatles to accompany them as a warm up at their 1996 concert at Earl's Court; The Bon Jovi Experience have performed with none other than Bon Jovi himself and T-Rextasy have shared the stage with several members of the original T-Rex band as well as the late Marc Bolan's son, Rolan.

Artist or Craftsman? Making the Faustian Bargain

If they are good enough for the originals, why aren't they good enough for the critics? Rather than questioning the validity of imitative art, and bewailing the fact that this area of the music industry is expanding, it might be better to reflect more objectively on the usefulness of imitative performance to musicians and the industry. First and foremost, the suggestion that if only the tribute acts would down tools then the stages of festivals, pubs and auditoriums which they currently occupy would be filled by the truly talented original musicians, is wildly utopian. It denies the realities of professional practice in an industry, where, as Fairley (2001: 273) points out, "musicians have all their lives had to struggle to earn a living from their craft," and where, "the tension between making [their] own music and locating an audience has always affected choice of repertoire, arrangement and style." Musicians are regularly faced with a difficult choice between living precariously while maintaining a high level of autonomy and creative freedom, or surrendering their liberty in exchange for financial stability. The insecurity and unpredictable working conditions of the industry have driven hardened idealists to make the Faustian bargain of joining a tribute or cover act. However in doing so they cross a longstanding line, artificially drawn between artists and craftsmen, a barrier which separates physical labour from mental toil. This division, which underpins critiques of imitative art practice in the broadest sense, can be traced back to the Renaissance where a distinction was created between artists and craftsmen as the concept of the "celebrity artist" first emerged. Most medieval craftsmen were employed by the church and perceived to be quite low down the social scale but opportunities presented by private patronage, allowed a new breed of artists to establish themselves as a superior, more cerebral category of practitioner. Georgio Vasari's pioneering biographies of contemporary artists give some indication of the status and mystique newly attached to their identity. On the subject of Michelangelo's capabilities, he is less than measured:

> The most benevolent Ruler of Heaven ... decided in order to rid us of so many errors, to send to earth a spirit who, working alone, was able to demonstrate in every art and every profession the meaning of perfection in the art of design, how to give relief in painting by proper drawing, lines, shading and light, how to work with good judgement in sculpture, and how to make buildings comfortable and secure, healthy, cheerful, well-proportioned, and richly adorned with various decorations in architecture. Moreover, He wanted to join to this spirit true moral philosophy and the gift of sweet poetry, so that the world would admire and prefer him for the wholly singular example of his life, his work, the holiness of his habits, and all his human undertakings, and so that we would call him something divine rather than human. (Vasari, 1998: 414)

Vasari's hyperbolic inflation of the role of the artist may seem absurd but in a less florid manner, elevation of the status of artists *vis-à-vis* craftsmen continues to the present day and the division is now stubbornly fixed. Efforts have been made to reunite art with the crafts in a bid to reaffirm the importance of craftsmanship, but these have floundered under the weight of importance attached to fine art practice. In the first quarter of the twentieth century for example, Walter Gropius in his role as head of the internationally acclaimed Bauhaus design school, attempted to draw the two professions back together insisting in his opening speech that, "There is no essential difference between the artist and the craftsman," but the fact that he went on to describe the artist as an "elevated" craftsman, did little to affect the status quo.[5] As the century progressed, the emphasis on art as an unfettered cerebral process continued to cement the downgrading of the manual component of artistic expression. As a consequence, craft skills and craft practitioners remain undervalued.

Taking a lead from the visual arts, a similar degree of creative snobbery pervades the aesthetics of popular music particularly when it comes to judgements regarding the worth of the industry's craftsmen – cover, tribute and session musicians – all of whom are relegated to the critical third division. The criteria for evaluation remain tantalizingly vague, as the status of particular performers varies enormously among critics and over time. Subjectivity and taste as much as any fully articulated aesthetic or musical criteria, are the main indices of value judgements. Although the work of cover, tribute and session musicians is an essential aspect of the industry, it is treated as though it were invisible – channels of recognition are very limited and the public are generally unaware of the significance of the contribution made by the hidden workforce. The impact of this disregard is tangible. In a recent documentary on tribute bands, Wayne Ellis articulates the thoughts of many of his co-workers. Reflecting on his subordinate status as bass player and frontman in a Thin Lizzy tribute band, he laments, "I always describe myself as an entertainer, which disappoints me. I wanted to be a true artist." In rejecting the significance of performance, Ellis effectively affirms the lower value placed on craft skills. In a similar vein, musician Howie Gudgeon bemoans the lack of opportunities for personal creativity in his professional life performing the music and identity of Angus Young in the AC/DC tribute, AB/CD, complaining bluntly that, "Music is a creative art, being a copyist is not."[6] Comments like these indicate that practitioners collude with critics by negating the value of their own performance skills. In doing so, they appear to have internalized the myth of unlimited creativity, a discourse which obscures the music industry's longstanding commitment to copying and imitation. Regardless of whether it is a superior or inferior activity, imitation pervades the history of popular music – a point emphasized by Plasketes, who writes of how:

> Standardization, interpretation, incorporation, adaptation, appropriation and appreciation have been manifest in a multitude of musical manners and methods, including retrospectives and reissues, the emergence of rap and sampling as commercially dominant pop styles, karaoke, and a steady flow, if not stream, of cover compilations and

> tribute recordings which revisit a significant cross section of musical periods, styles, genre and artists and their catalogs of compositions. (Plasketes, 2005: 137)

Few artists could claim absolute originality: amongst countless examples of imitation and re-interpretation, are some which have led to lengthy, legal battles regarding ownership. The ensuing court cases demonstrate that the creation of something entirely original is nothing like as straightforward as it might seem, a point elaborated by Voltaire's who wrote that: "Originality is nothing by judicious imitation. The most original writers borrowed one from another." Whether the theft is open, as is the case in the postmodern practice of sampling, or if it is carried out on a subconscious level, artists cannot help being influenced by one another. It does seem though that with regards the legal tussles surrounding authorship, when it comes to popular music, concerns regarding the aesthetic value of original compositions are far outweighed by anxieties over potential loss of earnings. In Garofalo's (1999: 318) words, this is because, "Like any culture industry in a market economy, the role of the music business is fundamentally to transform its cultural products into financial rewards." Capitalism only attaches value to creativity when it is profitable and attitudes to copying and imitation simply reflect the industry's overriding ideology. When it suits commercial purposes and if a financial incentive is involved both practices are condoned and exercised shamelessly.

Copying in a Commercial Context

The history of the cover song illustrates changing attitudes to the concept of originality and the impact of this on the respective status of artists and songwriters over time. It also shows how the value of individual cultural products is dependent on prevailing market forces and the organization of the industry. In the early days of radio, few people were able to play pre-recorded music at home. Therefore, at this time, a recording artist's main function was to disseminate contemporary songs with a view to increasing sales of the industry's primary product – sheet music. For although a minority could afford to buy records, far more consumers could be depended upon to purchase the printed form. With sales of sheet music as the main criteria for success if a variety of artists offered different recorded versions of the same song, so much the better. Furthermore it should be taken into account that singers did not as a rule write their own music or lyrics as standard practice dictated that this was the role of the professional songwriter. The profession of song plugging provides valuable insights into the music industry's priorities and the strategies used to promote song popularity. In a study of the life and work of the legendary songwriter Jimmy McHugh, Shipton (2009: 21) describes the role of the indefatigable song pluggers who, "Each working for a different publisher ... would make the rounds of the salons and ice-cream parlors where music was played, offering their latest songs for performance." Pluggers would move relentlessly across the towns and cities, seeking out bars and saloons where their songs could be played live to ensure maximum interest was generated. McHugh, who began his career playing light classics and contemporary hits in a Boston ice cream parlour, where live music was employed to draw in crowds from the nearby train station, was regularly approached by pluggers.

> They would plug any place where there was a group of people. They'd walk in, go right into their song, and maybe do one other number and then out. Then another plugger from another firm would come in ... I would interrupt my mind only to play for them, and then, goodbye! In the winter, I joined the industrious little horde of pluggers scurrying about he city like pilgrims, dedicated to the cause of implanting popular songs upon the mind of America. (McHugh quoted in Shipton 2009: 21)

Having experienced plugging in his role as an entertainer, he was fully aware of its importance in the promotion of new music and used his insider knowledge when he turned to songwriting to maximize the sales of sheet music for his own compositions.

With the growth of the record industry, sales of the printed variety were threatened by the recorded medium. Before World War Two, the record industry was relatively stable, dominated by a few major companies and a limited number of well-known artists who were famous mainly for their radio and screen performances. After the war record sales accelerated and with the help of A&R professionals who were able to match artists to repertoire, performers were able to operate across the previously separate worlds of radio, film and the record industry.[7] These changes are reflected in the documentation of success hierarchies. When the record industry was in its infancy, trade magazines measured the popularity of songs according to the number of different versions currently in circulation. If we look at early copies of *Billboard* for example, the "Honor Role of Hits," lists subsequent covers below the first recording of a song and, according to Belz (1970: 18) during the early 1950s: "A typical chart, would show the 25 most popular records in the country. Of that number, however, two or three versions of the same song were frequently found among the top ten records." There were major variations in style and delivery between the different renditions of popular songs and connotations of inferiority were not associated with the practice since essentially, they were not guilty of copying a definitive version.[8]

The White Face of Black Music: Race Covers

With the growth of consumer culture and the arrival of affordable record players, by the 1950s sheet music sales were eclipsed by record sales so that in the 1960s, "Record sales surpassed the gross revenues of all other forms of entertainment" (Peterson and Berger 1975: 167). When rock'n'roll records became the dominant musical product, the practice of copying was again mobilized to enable white artists to make cover versions of songs originally recorded by black and country musicians. While black rock'n'roll artists continued the musical traditions of blues and jazz by writing and performing their own material, their white counterparts relied on the services of Tin Pan Alley. However, in order to market black "underground" music to the widest possible audience, the music industry created sanitized cover versions to avoid offending the racially segregated audiences of the day.[9] A white group or soloist was called upon to perform a song already recorded by a black artist on one of the low-circulation record labels associated with black music. By offering acceptable "white" versions of a song, these "cross-cover" records were able to secure a larger share of the market than the smaller "race music" labels but before long, the copies supplanted their archetypes and many consumers had no knowledge of the music's original source. The vocal artist Pat Boone, epitomized the acceptable white face of black music during the 1950s. His chart successes included *Ain't That a Shame*, a version of a record originally recorded by Fats Domino and covers of the Little Richard songs *Long Tall Sally* and *Tutti Frutti* amongst others. Although the practice declined as white artists began to write their own material, the covering of pop songs did not automatically expire, and even during the 1960s, multiple renditions of the popular songs of the day made it difficult to establish a "definitive" version.

Individualism and the New Rock Aesthetic

As popular music matured, various sub-genres evolved giving rise to a set of competing discourses concerning the importance attached to both originality and authorship. In particular, the emergence of a rock aesthetic led to a volte-face concerning originality, when the concept of the rock performer as creative auteur was used to distinguish rock from the less cerebral, pop music.[10] The conflation of the artist with notions of individuality and the appearance of the auteur surfaced in conjunction with a new breed of singer-songwriters in the 1960s and early 1970s. During this period, a number of country and folk inspired musicians including Bob Dylan, Donovan, Leonard Cohen and Joni Mitchell defined themselves, or were defined by others, as popular music authors. At the same time, further cementing the close connection between author and performance, other artists, who had previously worked purely in a songwriting capacity (as did Neil Diamond and Carol King for example), began to operate instead, as performers of their own work.

Along with the elevation of the author, music's role as a vehicle for the expression of shared meanings began to give way to a more private mode of consumption and the construction of a pseudo-personal relationship between artist and audience. The first-person confessional style of the singer-songwriters celebrated the importance of the individual, while promoting the concept of the text as a channel to the artist's innermost psyche – a development which taps into the audience's subconscious desire to connect with the author. In popular music, this desire is expressed through the widespread preference for songs over instrumentals. As Frith (1987: 97) explains; unlike the more impersonal instrumental track, through the medium of song, the individual voice is able to personalize music. Vocalizing and the unique qualities of the voice are essential vehicles for the expression of the important elements of meaning and personality. In Willis' words, "The sound of a voice and all the extra-linguistic devices used by singers, such as vocal inflections, nuances, hesitations, emphases or sighs, are just as important in conveying meaning as explicit statements, messages and stories" (quoted in Waldrep 2004: 115). Singer songwriter Robyn Hitchcock, expands these thoughts in a reflection on the relationship between Bob Dylan's voice and the listener:

> what makes him so compelling to those of us he compels, is that he discovered a voice that no one had before. He came up with a new way of singing, which has influenced so many from Lennon to Lou Reed to me. Like a baby crying, he's hard to ignore. You don't put Dylan on in the background to make the party swing; either you give him your full attention, or like a crying baby, the sound he makes is maddening. But he keeps you company You put on a Dylan record and, by God, you know someone else Is there with you. It is a corrosive voice, restless, inconsolable, eating through the excuses that humanity feeds itself on. (Hitchcock, 2006: 9)

The constructed view of music as a medium of personal expression is partly responsible for the negative evaluation of imitative performance. Conditioned to the idea that we have a direct relationship with the artist via their presence, in live performance or on record, we perceive any alternative mode of delivery as inferior. An imitation of another's work regardless of its quality, is only of value if it bears the stamp of an identified virtuoso. This aura of mystique fulfils corporate objectives for although pop and rock fans are conditioned to conflate authenticity and worth with the presence of an identifiable songwriter or performer, notions of individualism ultimately serve the industry's purposes by providing an illusion of choice and self-determinism. Individuality's primary function in the music industry is little more than a corporate tool for differentiating artists one from another for inflating financial reward.

Mind over Matter – Composition vs. Performance

The elevation of composition helped to deepen the dichotomy between the more cerebral process of creating original music and its physical realization through means of performance. This is clearly inscribed within copyright laws which exist to protect the physical expression of authored ideas. In practice, the mental work of composition is protected if it achieves physical form in the shape of sheet music or a recording and in some circumstances, regardless of whether the work has been officially registered, protection can occur at the point of creation with ownership being assigned to the originator of that work. In the US since the Copyright Act of 1976, ownership of music belongs in the first instance, to the composer and is in force the moment a composition is "fixed in any tangible medium of expression"[11] such as on paper or as a computer file. There are of course, exceptions, the ownership may for example, be transferred to another group or individual and due to the financial benefits conferred by copyright, there is a lengthy history of disputes regarding competing claims to authorship. In one example, similarities between George Harrison's hit song *My Sweet Lord* (1970) and an earlier song by the American vocal harmony group, The Chiffons, led to a dispute over composition rights which took many years and numerous twists and turns, to resolve. *He's So Fine* was originally recorded in 1963 and it was eventually acknowledged in court that Harrison's use of the melody constituted plagiarism, albeit potentially unconsciously motivated. Some years later in 2006, Matthew Fisher, organist and founder member of the 1960s rock group Procul Harum, won a battle over his contribution to the hit record *A Whiter Shade of Pale* (1967). It was argued in court, that his distinctive melody established the song's identity and was therefore an essential aspect of its subsequent success.[12]

With the introduction of performing rights, authors have access to an additional slice of the cake, in that they can gather revenue from live and broadcast performances of their work. By contrast performers, the musical equivalent of the proletariat, are offered little protection for their labours unless they play their own compositions for, as Toynbee (in Frith 2004: 124) points out, the law set up a system of value which deems performance as an inferior practice. This means that whilst the creative output of songwriters is protected, those who devote their lives to performance are seen to have produced nothing of worth. The legally inscribed inferiority of performance and the elevation of mind over body imply that to perform anything other than one's own material is symptomatic of creative bankruptcy. In practice, those who choose to enter the world of tribute entertainment are doubly discredited. First by making a living out of performance rather than composition, they are automatically designated to the lower ranks, while their decision to perform someone else's repertoire, only amplifies the inferiority of their status.

The elevation of composition can only occur within a culture which privileges mind over body and the literary above the oral. Drew (2001: 51) notes the impact of this prejudice on the career of Elvis Presley, who notwithstanding his phenomenal success in terms of record sales, struggled to achieve acceptance as a serious artist. Even though his performance skills were outstanding, his failure to write his own work had a detrimental effect on the critical reception of his work. In the words of critic Jon Landau (quoted in Frith 1983: 53), "the criterion of art in rock is the capacity of the musician to create a personal, almost private, universe and to express it fully" and although Elvis delivered songs with passion and sensitivity, by using his body as a primary instrument he was essentially viewed more as a musical labourer than a distinguished auteur.

Emphasis on the concept of music as an expression of personal interiority relates to an earlier Romantic tradition established by nineteenth century artists reacting to the pressure to conform to industrialization and marketplace economics. United in their efforts to protect the status of cultural production by separating it from craftsmanship, Romantics endorsed the individual artist's imagination as the pinnacle of critical authority (whether or not this conflicted with the ideology of mass production). Although the Romantic aesthetic fits awkwardly with the commercial goals of the post-war music industry, it continues to underpin much of the thinking around the exclusivity of creativity which legitimates a hierarchy of musicianship. While the writer Edgar Allen Poe and the painter James Whistler may have launched an uncompromising defence of the pursuit of art for its own sake, for the vast majority of practitioners, such intransigence is untenable – books, paintings and records must be sold or financial support will be withdrawn. Creativity by itself, will not pay the rent. Moreover, as already noted, the creative process itself, is not inexhaustible as: "When musicians or singers produce innovation in music they have to do so by modifying and adapting forms with which they are already familiar" (Wall 2003: 21). Improvisation may be tolerated in jazz circles but mainstream popular music is much more dependent on recognizable song structures and easily absorbed lyrics, many of which bear resemblance one to another. When it comes to popular taste, audiences generally prefer familiarity over avant garde art practice.

The True Cost of Imitation

Leaving aside any aesthetic arguments, copies pose a particular threat to the authority of the canon – this is particularly the case if the reproduction of the original text is too adept. It is easy enough for critics to deride a poor quality copy, but credible imitations are feared because of their potential impact on the economic value of the cultural product being copied. Fakes are normally perceived as an unwelcome visitor within the academy and the marketplace since they have the ability to deceive and ultimately, they can undermine the worth of art objects. In the market for fine arts for example, the faking of artworks is particularly problematic. On the one hand art historians are concerned with the threat they present to the unique aura of the original, while legal experts see them as capable of undermining ownership and potential profit. High profile fakes are capable of disrupting the very foundations of a value system constructed around the judgements of critics who earn a living from assigning value to individual artworks. If they can't tell the good from the bad, how are we to know the difference between Old Master and Young Pretender and who should we trust when purchasing a painting or a print? The widespread nature of the practice and its derogatory impact on the value of collectibles has led to a vast body of academic and popular enquiry.[13] The focus of the work relates primarily to the value of objets d'art, but the overriding arguments are equally relevant in the field of popular music where authorship and identity are similarly conflated.

In popular music circles, the knowledge and opinions of experts and critics are challenged by the skills of the industry's craftsmen – session musicians and those employed in tribute and cover bands. These individuals have the skill needed to create a convincing "fake" and yet, this degree of ability is normally assigned solely to artists imbued with canonic status. Since critics must demonstrate their ability through identifying the superior text or performance, anything which threatens the omnipotence of the original seriously undermines their authority. Therefore, within hierarchies of merit, a first-class Beatles' tribute must always be second-rate, regardless of the levels of musicianship and interpretive ability displayed. The frightening idea that a copy may be of superior technical quality cannot even be countenanced. Following the tradition of the art world, where the value of paintings is dependent on their authentication and attribution to a particular artist, a similar formula ascribes recognized works of excellence to acknowledged virtuosos.

The rock genre in particular, allows virtuosity to play a primary role in determining who is worthy of canonical status – the classic values of rock centre upon its ability to communicate directly with the audience and any deviation from this tradition must be challenged. During the 1980s, for example, the popularity of the "synthpop" phenomenon with its celebration of the artificial, countered rock's value system. The threat posed by the genre's electronically generated sounds, impersonal vocals and mechanical rhythms quickly led to a backlash and a reinstatement of rock's core values. As Middleton (1990: 90) puts it: "In the context of the synthesizer bands prevalent in the early 1980s, the work of committed guitar-based performers, like Big Country, U2 and Bruce Springsteen, was actively taken to signify commitment to the 'classic' values of rock."

The credibility of the canon rests on public acceptance of virtuosos, a limited number of key players, whose status has been cemented through a combination of critical markers such as, public opinion, peer and industry approval. Guitarist, songwriter and performer Eric Clapton's elevation to canonic status, illustrates how the process works. During the 1960s, Clapton was a respected musician who worked in several bands – notably the Yardbirds and Cream. Soon however, his powers of musicianship were mythologized, leading some to bestow him with divine status, particularly after the slogan "Clapton is God" was spray painted on a wall in an Islington underground station by a fan. The message then spread to other areas of the UK as the process of canonization continued. Clapton went on to receive further public acknowledgement through a number of channels such as induction into the Rock and Roll Hall of Fame where he was accepted on three separate occasions.[14] Other accolades include Grammy awards for vocal and instrumental performance, BAFTA, BMI and MTV nominations for television and film music.

Clapton is also regularly voted as an outstanding performer in popular opinion polls. Through public acknowledgement like this, his status as a performer and songwriter is assured and by a process of exclusion, the prodigious talents of equally gifted musicians are routinely overlooked.

Standing in the Shadows: the Session Artists

Unlike the official rock gods, and despite being showcased on important song recordings and providing instrumental support on tours, most session musicians have until quite recently, received very little in the way of public recognition. Due to the conflation of music and identity, the identification of a named individual is key to the attribution of any cultural value to recordings. In one of the few studies devoted to the status of freelance music workers, Frederickson and Rooney (2005) noted how session artists experience a similar level of "non-personhood" to other low status workers identified by the sociologist Erving Goffman (1956) in his seminal study of the meanings of human action. Where Goffman linked this invisibility to skill limitations in an increasingly mechanized society, their study found the obscurity of skilled freelance musicians was defined, more by a lack of access to power and creative decision-making than it was to a skills deficit. Although skilled and professional in other respects, session workers do not usually belong to an established, named, artistic group and are not therefore perceived as "present" in recordings. Furthermore, in live performances, their stage presence may be sidelined for, as Frederickson and Rooney (2005: 223) contend, "the dramaturgical organization in the theatre symbolizes and affirms [the] role conflict between core and support personnel."

Heard but not necessarily seen, the contribution made by this professional corps to popular music, is shrouded in anonymity, making the labour equally inconspicuous. For these reasons, the public is generally unaware of the significance of the role of session artists in determining both the content and quality of key recordings and performances. During the 1960s for example, few knew the extent of Jimmy Page's session work which, according to Santoro (1995: 72) encompassed, "doing constant session-guitar work for everyone from the Kinks and Stones to Donovan and Jackie DeShannon." The guitarist Duane Allman was another who worked on various recordings as a session musician. Both prior to and during his career with The Allman Brothers band the acclaimed musician supported many high-profile artists, notably Otis Redding, Aretha Franklin and King Curtis and his contribution to Eric Clapton's song *Layla* is now acknowledged as fundamental to the recording's phenomenal success.[15] In contrast to the majority of session workers, Page and Allman went on to become household names as artist's in their own right, at which point their session work was eventually acknowledged and in 2000, the Rock and Roll Hall of Fame finally introduced the category of "Sideman" to its induction list, thus allowing the work of a very limited number of hitherto unknown session players to receive public acclaim. More recently, the contribution of the hidden workforce is recognized in documentary films such as *Standing in the Shadows of Motown* (2003) and *Respect Yourself: The Story of Stax Records* (2007), both of which celebrate the work of those session musicians responsible for the creation of legendary soul sounds of the 1960s. This kind of public acknowledgement addresses the marginalized musicianship and at last puts a face to the anonymous session workers.

Without identification then, musicians' labours go unnoticed and yet in popular music circles, the issue of identity is somewhat problematic. Consistent identities are difficult to maintain when ego battles, alcohol and substance abuse are combined with occupational insecurity, long hours and a family unfriendly ethos – all of which make it very difficult for individuals or groups to sustain a consistent career, let alone a fixed identity. Enduring identity is not consistent with a creative industry defined by a commitment to continual change either. This is particularly the case in the culture of pop music where reinvention has become an industry leitmotif.[16] Perhaps because the trials and tribulations of touring and media intrusion drive many acts to implode, regroup or permanently disband, the fragile nature of identity inflates the premium placed upon it?

Me and My Shadow: Original Artists and Their Tributes

Doomed to occupy the lower rungs of hierarchies of aesthetic merit, damned and derided by critics, ignored by the canon but does the work of the imitators offer anything of value, particularly to the archetypes and if so, what are their thoughts on the parodic workforce? The response of original artists varies enormously – far from being aggrieved, some of them heap praise on their disciples. American rock legend Aerosmith's endorsement of their favoured tribute Draw the Line, allows the band the privilege of advertising themselves as the only one officially endorsed by the original: unlike their rivals, through an unwritten agreement, they are even allowed to use Aerosmith's logos and slogans.[17]

Aerosmith's magnanimity towards their tributes is matched by Morrissey's as regards his own flock. According to Jose Maldonado (ersatz Morrissey of Californian Smiths tribute The Sweet and Tender Hooligans), he and the band have received glowing testimonies from their exemplar.

> Morrissey himself has seen a couple of our performances and gave us good praise. I appear in his video for "Irish Blood, English Heart" and on a couple of occasions, he's jokingly announced to his audiences at his concerts – "Hello, we are the Sweet and Tender Hooligans ... I am Jose." (Jose Maldonado, email, September 2007)

For any musician, praise like this is highly sought after but the chance to play before the original artist must surely be one of the greatest privileges. In the case of Australian Pink Floyd, the transcendent moment occurred when they were invited to play at David Gilmour's fiftieth birthday party in 1996. The ultimate accolade though, has to be an invitation to play with the real band, an honour bestowed upon The Australian Floyd's guitarist and founder Steve Mac, who was invited to join Pink Floyd's Roger Waters on a world tour.[18]

Presumably artists like Morrissey and The Pink Floyd recognize the benefits of free promotion and payments for copyrighted music they will no doubt receive from venues licensed to play live music. Add to this the potential earnings from compilations of re-released material which the tribute bands continually keep alive in the popular imagination, and it is easy to see the merits of attracting an army of impersonators. The symbiotic relationship can even help to re-launch a fading artist's career as happened in the case of ABBA and their tribute Bjorn Again (Figure 6.2).

Figure 6.2 Bjorn Again, performing the greatest hits of Abba (photograph Rod Stephen, by permission)

ABBA broke up during the early 1980s, at a time when tribute bands were much thinner on the ground than they are now and in 1988 their most successful tribute ever was formed. According to Bjorn Again's manager Rod Leissle, the members of ABBA were generally supportive of his stage show, despite being mystified as to why anyone would still be interested in their music. However, following a lengthy hiatus, songwriters Bjorn Ulvaeus and Benny Andersson were quick to exploit the potential of their imitators when they decided to release *ABBA Gold* in 1992. At the time their original albums had been off the market for a number of years and recognizing the practical and emotional difficulties they would face in any attempt to reunite the original band for a tour, they invited Bjorn Again to go on television to promote the new compilation. Ulvaeus even sent the band a telegram saying that anyone who resembled him deserved a successful career – probably never imagining that the tribute's lifespan in performance would eventually outlive ABBA's own career! This example demonstrates very clearly, that there are opportunities for a win-win situation if all parties co-operate and in this case, where Bjorn Again essentially acted as ambassadors for ABBA, the symbiotic potential was exploited to maximum effect.

Similar instances of these reciprocal relationships abound. One observer in an internet newsgroup, refuting the argument that imitative artists are essentially parasites, suggests instead that they offer opportunities for a mutual benefit. Citing the example of the David Bowie tribute, The Jean Genie who had recently played a concert in Dublin she writes:

> One of the radio stations here chose to mark the event by playing Bowie's back catalogue throughout the day. This blitz of airplay for his early '70s stuff to coincide with Jean Genie being in town was very timely for Bowie, as he had "Best of 69/74" in the charts at the same time. Jean Genie were essentially promoting it for him. (Dara, Alt.Fan. David-Bowie, posted 2 April 1998)

In this case the various parties – radio station, original and tribute artists and fans – all stood to benefit and as the writer points out, David Bowie in particular, would be the prime beneficiary of the communal effort. Perhaps because they are flattered or prefer to see the potential benefits offered, the most magnanimous famous artists may opt to embrace the entire parodic flock. Instead of rejecting the imitators, they offer them the ultimate accolade by referring to them as "favourites" or endorsing them as "official" tributes, conferring the elite status through acknowledgements on their websites. At the time of writing for example, the official KISS website contains no less than 100 such bands who are proudly referred to as: The KISS Army.[19]

Star Wars

Although a sizeable proportion of those paying homage are clearly devoted to their prototypes, and as we have seen the love may be mutual, but as we all know, the course of true love seldom runs smoothly and this is certainly so in the case of those who devote their lives to performing somebody else's identity. For a minority, hero worshipping pays off (in economic terms at least), even to the extent that the imitators make more money than the originals (Tarlach 2002). For this reason, certain artists may be less than happy to share their identity or any financial gains to be made from it. Performing rights only ensure an income stream derived from the live performances of music and although copyright laws protect recordings and sheet music, identity is much less easy to protect. As we tend to take our identities as a given, we don't ponder on what makes them unique. There are a few precedents – for instance, it is acknowledged that legal rights can be attributed to a distinctive vocal style. In a case against a Bette Midler tribute, the court ruled that: "A voice is as distinctive and personal as a face. The human voice is one of the most palpable ways identity is manifested" and, "the singer manifests herself in the song."[20] Taking this into account, to impersonate Midler or any other well-known artist's voice, is an act of identity theft. but when it comes to individual mannerisms and styles of dress, it is perhaps more difficult to prove that these belong unequivocally, to specific individuals. However, in the light of the modern preoccupation with celebrity identities and the ease with which they can be recycled post-internet, the concept of an economic value being attached to identity is increasingly recognized.

Needless to say, the higher the profile of an original artist, the greater the sum attached to their identity and the more concern to protect it from exploitation. In a particularly high-profile case against the producer of the stage show *Beatlemania*, an award of $7.5 million was won by The Beatles' company Apple, based on what was seen as, "reasonable value of what the defendant [had] taken."[21] The detailed production made use of sound and look-alike imitators who gave a live performance of 29 Beatles' songs, accompanied by slides and related imagery. As the show ran from 1977–1979 and then toured the US before going worldwide, the sum awarded was felt to be a fair estimate of a share of the potential revenue from licence fees, performances, and the film of the stage show. The *Beatlemania* show, by copying the looks, fashions and mannerisms of The Beatles, clearly infringed the rights of publicity, which exist to enable individuals and groups to control their identity. In the court's opinion, the show violated The Beatles' publicity rights because the audience, "fell prey to the illusion that they were actually viewing The Beatles in performance."[22] For renowned artists like The Beatles, it is relatively easy to prove the connection between artist and identity but tributes to lesser artists, have also found their pursuit of second-hand fame leading to litigation and in some circumstances, the costs are significant. A successful case was brought against Madness tribute, Ultimate Madness, who were ordered to pay a high price for recreating the famous walk used by the original artists in performances of the song, *One Step Beyond.* Brother of the inventor of the walk, Brendan Smyth, claimed copyright and despite the fact that it was only being used for five minutes during the Ultimate's show, he asked to be paid £100 every time they used it. Since this represented 50 per cent of the band's £200 nightly earnings, their act would no longer be viable if they continue to perform the walk.[23]

In the aforementioned case, the trademark walk was considered an inseparable, extra-musical aspect of the original act's identity and therefore belonged solely to Madness. Effectively, winning the dispute gives them the right to derive an income from anyone else who attempts to reiterate the walk while performing their work, but it is difficult to imagine where this might lead if all pop and rock artists were subjected to similar legal challenges. When it comes to stage presence, what debt does New York Doll's David Johansen owe to Mick Jagger; did Billy Fury cash in on Elvis Presley's flamboyant image by copying his gold lame stage suits and pelvic thrusts and if so, to what extent did he benefit financially? More recently we might ask who inspired Morrissey's hairstyle? Did he steal his trademark quiff from Fury, as rumour has it, but if he did, surely Fury's rockabilly style was inspired by Elvis in the first place? Clearly this is a problematic legal field and although successful cases have been launched and won, it is all too easy for the tribute act to make minor adjustments to logos, stage outfits and style in order to continue performing.

Alternative Critiques

Original artists are clearly embroiled in a love/hate relationship with their tributes and critics only regurgitate well-trodden complaints regarding creative deficit and economic freeloading, but the skill involved in copying and adaptation is rarely considered and can never be addressed within critiques which consider imitation to be an entirely worthless or parasitic practice. The pre-eminence of the original over the copy and composition over performance, automatically places musicians on the cover and tribute scene at a disadvantage but performance is an essential aspect of their identity. Since the will to perform propels many to take on an alien identity in the first place, and as there is little call for recorded cover versions by unknown amateurs or semi-professionals, live performance remains their primary means of establishing any worth. Struggling to identify anything of value in reiteration, critics are further hampered by their preoccupation with the significance of original recordings and performances. Understandably, applying these frameworks makes it difficult to ascertain anything of value in a tribute, however, with a different set of evaluative tools, there are alternatives to the predominant critique.

If we start by looking to non-Western cultures, imitative art is viewed somewhat differently. In a study of that ultimate imitative practice, karaoke, Drew (2001: 19) demonstrates that our preoccupation with originality is not universally shared. He explains how the Japanese view imitation in a much more positive light, identifying purpose and value in copying as part of a "necessary phase in the acquisition of many valued cultural skills." In the Japanese martial arts, calligraphy and flower arrangement, careful copying is promoted to encourage the internalization of the mystical "way" of an art form. Here, the practice of imitation is the very essence of a cultural continuity which strives to preserve rules and traditions in order to allow for extremely subtle expressions of creativity and originality. Karaoke for example, encourages singers to pursue the traditional practice of imitation by copying the minor nuances of a song and adhering carefully to the original text. By learning the song in this way, the issue of originality is elided as the would-be performer accepts the authority of the original in preparation for their own subtle deviation from it. In order to appreciate karaoke, the uniqueness of the performance needs to be appreciated and enjoyed in its own right and the value of the performer's work rests more on the discipline they display in perfecting the original text and any unique refinements they bring to it. If the same approach is applied to pop homage, it seems an appropriate way to appreciate the positive qualities of a carefully prepared tribute, since it accepts minor deviations from the original, as well as the tremendous skill involved in recreating a complex or well-known repertoire.

This seems a positive way forward – any blunt dismissal of imitation will be unable to acknowledge, let alone recognize, the delicate nuances of performance which distinguish one tribute act from another but as Taruskin (1995) points out, performance is essentially an act and should not be viewed as a text. Performance is the raison d'être of the live tribute, so, rather than judging a tribute as the failed execution of a text, it is more constructive to appreciate the individuality of single performances, the responses of the audience and the diversity of approaches within the process. The human component and real-time setting ensure that each act and each event is unique, and in this sense, the performance contains an element of the aura which Benjamin ascribed to original artworks untainted by mass-production. Schechner (2006) argues that performances are actions, and with this in mind, critics should focus their attention less on the reiteration of a static text and more on the meanings generated by the performance. This dynamic approach places greater emphasis on music as an inherently social phenomenon and within this context, the travesty of simulation is replaced by an appreciation of the power of individual performances and their ability to generate unique meanings. Furthermore, it contrasts with Shoenberg's derogatory view of the performer as, "totally unnecessary except as his interpretations make the music understandable to an audience unfortunate enough not to be able to read it in print" (quoted in Newlin 1980: 164), so while rock and pop can be appreciated as studio arts, this is not the only means by which the music can be judged. The boundaries established by the recording can be traversed as the art work becomes an event with an unpredictable outcome. In Cook's (2003: 205) words:

> the contemporary performance studies paradigm stresses the extent to which signification is constructed through the act of performance, and generally through acts of negotiation either between performers, or between them and the audience. In other words, performative meaning is understood in process, and hence by definition is irreducible to product.

Finally, when attempting to evaluate live reiteration in a more positive light, we could return to the ancient Greeks to consider the status they attached to the singers known as rhapsodes, whose job it was to perform epic poetry.[24] Although the same framework was used in each performance, their skill centred on their ability to use experience and ability to improvise and to adjust the content of the poem for the different audiences. As rhapsodes were able to add their own jokes and stories to the performance, their skills were much admired by contemporary audiences who saw them as inspired performers, not failed copyists. The rhapsode's mystical connection to the imaginative powers of the original writer of the poem, provided him with access to the divine source of that creativity. Socrates went so far as to suggest that the poets were connected by a chain of rings, which were attracted by a magnetic power, linking them ultimately, to the creative Muse, an affiliation he likened to an account of the stone of Heraclea's strange ability to:

> not only attracts iron rings, but [to impart] to them a similar power of attracting other rings; and sometimes you may see a number of pieces of iron and rings suspended from one another so as to form quite a long chain; and all of them derive their power of suspension from the original stone. (Plato, 535e)

Our modern-day tributes, like rhapsodes, compete with one another to give the best performance and might it be possible that they too, are touched by the presence of the musical Muse?

7 Fandom and Collective Participation

Inevitably, while carrying out the research for this book, I went to more than a few gigs. Realizing that my enjoyment of tributes may not be shared universally, I wanted to know why others choose to engage with imitative entertainment and what pleasures they experience with what, on the surface, is considered by so many to be a second-rate form of entertainment? I was curious to understand the audience response to different tributes to establish whether emotions are directed primarily towards the archetypal musicians. Wondering what relationships were forged with the tribute artists themselves, I wanted to see how fans engage with them on an emotional level. I was also keen to observe how members of the audience make use of imitative musical texts as a vehicle for experiencing or sharing feelings.

Studying the behaviour and attitudes of fans at these events involves entering relatively uncharted territory for as Curtis (1987) notes, audiences are one of the least studied aspects of popular music. While the consumption of classical music is conditioned by the genre's lengthy history, popular music is still relatively new to the academy and is only partially accepted within scholarly circles. Furthermore, because classical music is well-established within the school and university curriculum, responses to it are carefully conditioned, making the reactions and activities of the audience more predictable and stable.

Although in recent years there has been a shift away from textual analysis towards studies of the everyday consumption of popular culture, Hesmondhalgh (2002: 118) believes there are still, "surprisingly few substantial empirical studies of popular music audiences." Furthermore, when it comes to the reception of live music, research is even thinner on the ground because the main thrust of research has leant towards the analysis of record, CD and video consumption. In terms of a challenge, the live audience offers the researcher a much more elusive and inconsistent source of study. Unlike music's material products, tribute audiences are hard to evaluate quantitatively and while quantitative approaches offer a means of calculating taste and popularity they can tell us little about the social aspect of music consumption. A point elaborated by Negus (2001: 12) who says that:

> Official sales figures produced by the recording industry provide us with an increasingly limited and partial way of representing consumption patterns, and of understanding the music being created around the world because they prioritize individual purchases of legally manufactured products. They give no indication of the ways in which music is created and consumed in a variety of social settings.

Maybe because in-depth research is so limited, stereotypical assumptions regarding who consumes pop and rock music and how they go about it, are too readily made. At the crudest level, we are conditioned to associate rock and metal audiences with rituals of masculine bonding, while pop is conflated with femininity and fun. Fans of punk rock are inevitably expected to engage in agit-prop activities whereas we anticipate a less aggressive, more cerebral and sensitive response from fans to indie music. A study of fan stereotyping (Rentfrow and Gosling 2007: 306–326), did find a kernel of truth in the relationship between individual personality, fan behaviour and music preference, but there are dangers in anticipating particular sets of behaviours according to genre. Simplistic means of categorizing audiences in this manner are as limiting as the genre labels themselves, a point emphasized by Holt (2007: 3).

> Categories of popular music are particularly messy because they are rooted in vernacular discourse, in diverse social groups, because they depend greatly on oral transmission, and because they are destabilized by shifting fashions and the logic of modern capitalism. The music industry daily invents and redesigns labels to market musical products as new and/or authentic.

More sophisticated insight into the psychological aspect of audience behaviours is provided by the growing body of work on fans, some of which can be related to the consumption of music. According to Sandvoss (2005: 2), early studies of fan behaviour pathologized their activities, suggesting that they were responding to a social structure designed to deny them intimacy and a proper sense of identity or community. In this unhealthy environment fans unmet needs are displaced onto an alternative source – the object of their fandom.[1] The pathological view of fandom was subsequently superseded by approaches offering richer and more complex explanations for typical activities: rather than viewing them as psychological misfits, these studies show fans as active users of texts and independent creators of meanings (Fiske 1989; Jenkins 1991). This means that music lovers can be seen less as victims of a capitalist ploy to extract money in a value system where economic exchange is but one facet of a wider cultural economy.

When attempting to study popular music, one of the main deficiencies in existing research is the tendency to conflate the medium with youth, something which mitigates against a deeper understanding of the consumption of pop and rock by older consumers, many of whom participate in tribute events. This is emphasized by Hesmondhalgh (2002: 116) who argues that:

> because many books, articles and courses have treated popular music as a phenomenon almost entirely associated with "youth," the musical experience of other people, of different ages, and of young people who do not necessarily conform to prevailing conceptions of "youth" have been marginalised.

Undoubtedly music plays a major and formative role within the lives of young people. This finding was confirmed by British scholars working in the emergent field of cultural studies where both Dick Hebdige (1979) and Paul Willis (1978) went to great lengths to illustrate the relationship between music and the behaviour of young male mods, punks and bikers. While Hebdige interpreted British punks' use of the safety pin, Mohican hairstyle and manic dance style the Pogo, as symbolic statements, Willis detected a direct connection between loud rock music and the culture of young, male bikers. The application of these studies however, is limited to the temporal contexts of the period in question and a Zeitgeist and demography associated with a distinctive post-war youth cultural formation. Hebdige and his fellow researchers could not predict how music would be used by ageing members of the spectacular youth subcultures some 30 years on.

Research in cultural studies certainly uncovered a homology between music and youth but Hermes (1995: 16) warns us against approaches which privilege self-conscious and considered uses of media texts generally, due to the "fallacy of meaningfulness" they may create. It is all too easy to assume that *all* young people are making symbolic statements when they engage with music but what can such approaches tell us about the uses of music in everyday life and those who engage with music in an arbitrary or unintentional manner? Alternative studies which might throw light on the consumption of popular music by those falling outside the well-trodden parameters of youth subcultural studies, are slow to emerge. We should not therefore, approach the mixed-age audience for with too many assumptions. It would be presumptuous for example, to anticipate a time-honoured response to vintage music from young people encountering a text from distant temporal and social context for the first time.

Bearing in mind the methodological shortcoming of existing research, when it comes to studying the continuing consumption of pop music by the baby boom generation (many of whom are now fifty- to sixty-somethings who have no desire to let go of their attachment to certain "youthful" pursuits) the problems are more acute. This is particularly the case when, as Young (2001) contends, the youth denominator is itself in need of revision.

> The term "youth culture" is at best of historical value only, since the customs and mores associated with it have been abandoned by your actual young person. The point is that today's teenager is no longer promiscuous, no longer takes drugs, and rarely goes to pop concerts. He leaves all that to the over-25s. (Young, quoted in Bennett 2001: 156)

Unlike the academy, which lags behind in relating to post-youth and intergenerational consumption of popular music, the music industry has been quick to address its relationship with the changing demography. According to Redhead (1990) and Savage (1988) the record industry has adapted readily to declining numbers of teenagers by repackaging music to appeal to mixed age consumers. This is because it recognizes that young people no longer "own" popular music in the way they once did, and widening access to the concept of "youth" means that the young must now share music with their parents and possibly grandparents too. The live sector also capitalizes on demographic change and the nostalgia boom, taking full advantage of the demand for retro-rock by mobilizing the troops of musical tributes. Homan (2006: 88) suggests that the industry puts forth tried and trusted music as a means of "risk mitigation" in uncertain economic times where, by linking live retro music to other examples of heritage consumption, a pre-conditioned audience can be captured. In this sense, tributes to the dead and defunct are the live sector's equivalent to the record industry's formulaic money spinners – the Greatest Hits collections.

Approaching a Changing Audience

Leaving aside for a moment the changing nature of music consumption in a post-youth scenario, regardless of which methodology is used, it is accepted that studying how people consume music is problematic at the best of times. In Frith's (2004: 34) view, "While we can point to general patterns of pop use, the precise link (or homology) between sounds and social groups remains unclear." This may be true but with the reattribution of the "youth" descriptor, clear cut connections between tastes and age are ever more tenuous. Zuben (2001: 5), argues that, the retro mode of pop no longer connects solely to, "the world of an institutionalised pop history and discourse" and links instead, to, "aspects of the specific and situated pasts and presents of people." This means that while nostalgia entertainment has the capacity to re-ignite musical memories in the minds and bodies of older members of the audience, younger fans' relationship with the same music will be quite different. At the Glastonbudget festival of 2007, for example, the audience response to The Sex Pistols Experience could hardly be likened to that of fans, to the water-born performance of the archetypal ensemble in the year of the Queen's Silver Jubilee. During the hot, politically charged summer of 1976, the Sex Pistols subversive boat trip acted as a refreshing antidote to the day's official celebrations on 7 June when:

> Later that same evening ... a boat called the Queen Elizabeth, bearing the Sex Pistols and 200 fans and friends, was stopped by the police in mid-performance near the Houses of Parliament. Malcolm McLaren, their manager, and 10 other people were arrested when it docked. (Street Porter 2002)

Thirty-one years later, after two days of non-stop rain and gale force winds in the Leicestershire countryside, the Glastonbudget audience was more subdued (Figure 7.1).

Figure 7.1 Glastonbudget audience (photograph Kevin Ryan, by permission)

The sleepy pastoral surroundings failed to ignite any outbursts of anti-royalist sentiment from the good natured inter-generational audience and there were no arrests as the 5,000 plus crowd showed a gritty determination to enjoy themselves in spite of the elements. Erstwhile punks, some balding, paunchy and decidedly middle-aged, Mohicans pointing defiantly towards the blackening skies, rubbed shoulders with punk-curious teenagers and children. Johnny Rotter's opening cry " 'Allo London" led to a desultory shower of beer and spittle, as a few of the older punks launched into the Pogo. Younger audience members took their lead from the old guard, resulting a merry frenzy of lop-sided Pogo dancing, as old and young submitted to the carnivalesque atmosphere.

Of course, the meanings of music cannot remain static – socio-political change and the evolution of personal politics will evoke markedly different responses to songs outside their original context. On the subject of music as a political tool, Dunaway (quoted in Lull 1987: 36) contends:

> The politics of a piece of music are communicated by its time, performer and audience. Thus the most comprehensive definitions of political music would take into account its specific context: the communicative function of a particular work in a particular setting at a particular place in time.

Just as an individual performer's style and tradition communicate potentially different meanings to a song, the context and performance of a piece of music can have a bearing on this process: in a different context or different historical period, the politics of a piece of music may undergo radical transformation It seems absurd now that the BBC decided to ban the Johnny Ray's hit, *Such a Night* in 1954 due to its suggestion that a young couple may have spent the night together. Likewise, on its first airing, the incendiary potential of the Little Richard song *Tutti Frutti* (1955), forced record company officials to undertake a clean up of the original version in order to avert a moralist furore. The industry was compelled to veto any allusions to gay sex but 60 years on, the subtlety of the veiled references to alternative sexuality is largely lost on a post-Stonewall audience.[2]

Today's sexually aware youth would be equally hard-pressed to comprehend why a song like Loretta Lynn's *The Pill* was banned on US radio stations in the 1970s for speaking openly about the use of the oral contraceptive in a committed long-term relationship Moreover, after years of struggle for equal rights, many modern women interpret Tammy Wynette's emotional ballad *Stand By Your Man* (1968) as a masochistic call for a return to subjugation. Predictable responses and youth-centric assumptions must be abandoned when studying tribute events where as Homan (2006: 69) points out, the employment of music, media texts and historical moments, is "double coded." This means that the audience engages with "the historical narrative of the imitated," while simultaneously mobilizing their own personal experiences of the artist in question. The dynamic is further complicated by the history of the relationship they may have formed with the individual tribute act and with other tributes to the same artist. Taking into account these complexities how then should the audience for this type of entertainment be approached?

Ruddock (2007: 9) describing audience research as a "haphazard affair" at best, suggests that any study should take on board the multiplicity of conceptual and methodological approaches currently in circulation. Reflecting on Nowotny's (2003: 115) observations regarding the fragility of expertise and the limits in establishing "quick, clear solutions to social enigmas," he alludes to the value of ethnographic approaches. Ethnography certainly seems to offer researchers a versatile academic tool kit – it is difficult to imagine a better medium for exploring the complex dynamics of the tribute fan/performer and performer/star relationships across a wide range of genres. Unlike methodologies which insist on objectivity and detachment at all costs, a holistic approach combining first-hand observation and interviews, enables researchers to uncover the rich details of fan behaviour. These findings can then be linked to common themes across fandom and the consumption of popular culture, as a means of illuminating the meanings of typical behaviours and interactions. Using an ethnographic approach at tribute events I was able to transcend the stereotype of a stagnant, nostalgia-ridden music scene to uncover a rich and vibrant theatre of social action. Instead of deluded wannabes and undiscerning consumers, I found a fan-friendly environment where talented musicians and erudite fans experience an uncustomary degree of intimacy and equality. The proximity of musicians to the audience fosters close connections and opportunities for encounters which are normally out of bounds, allowing fans to experience agency and engagement. Here, they can initiate actions and activities or experiment with fantasies and desires, in a setting where instead of being ignored, their efforts stand a chance of being acknowledged.

By mingling with the audience at various events it was easier to gain first-hand experience of some of these encounters and the pleasures evoked by imitative performance. Whilst it is certainly possible to experience fandom in a solitary capacity, deliberately joining forces with others creates a point of departure for a multiplicity of social activities which cannot be achieved alone. As Jenkins (1992: 76) writes, participatory fandom, "is always shaped through input from other fans and motivated, at least partially, by a desire for further interaction with a larger social and cultural community." Engaging with the fans and performers as an observer as well as a participant, not only added to my enjoyment, but increased my understanding of the scene's nuances.

"It Takes Every Kind of People"

In trying to establish who spends time and money enjoying imitative live music I soon found that although certain audiences matched existing research findings, this level of consistency could not always be anticipated on the tribute scene. Perhaps more than anything, the scene illustrates the sheer diversity of the audience for popular music in the twenty-first century. For instance, audiences at metal concerts generally lived up to the in-depth genre studies of Weinstein (2000) and Walser (1993) in that there were more white and male fans at these events but the age range at some of the gigs I attended, was characteristically a lot broader than might be anticipated. Younger fans were frequently in attendance and I was surprised to find entire concerts deliberately aimed at the under-18s, more so, when the artists involved were performing the work of rock dinosaurs such as Led Zeppelin and Queen. Despite the fact that these archetypal virtuosos were entertaining the audiences' parents and grandparents some forty years earlier, the events were well attended. Children also appeared in the audience at concerts not aimed specifically for them, usually accompanied by parents, who seemed keen to share their love of 1960s and 1970s music with their offspring. At the other end of the spectrum, fans of pensionable age could be found, clearly enjoying the music of their youth alongside children and teenagers. Occasionally, I came across entire extended family groups, united by their shared love of music. Families were particularly visible at the outdoor festivals like Glastonbudget and Tribfest where the campsite provided alternative entertainment for younger children.[3]

These findings resonate with the observations of the bands I interviewed: Wanda Ortiz said that the The Iron Maidens attracted fans at the younger end of the age range. When asked who usually comes to see the band she said: "Although our audience seems to be comprised mostly of guys aged 18 to 38 we see quite a few women and younger teenagers (at our all-ages shows)" (Wanda Ortiz, email, May 2007). Jaymz of Beatallica also emphasized the broad age range of his band's audience, explaining that since their fans traverse the traditional genre boundaries of metal and pop, they are less predictable:

> We get both Beatles and Metallica fans at shows. The demographic ranges from 15 to 65 really. We try to use the band as sort of an educational medium ... turn Beatles' fans on to metal and show them metalheads aren't all dolts ... turn on Metallica fans to The Beatles and show them that their parents weren't that square after all ... The Beatles wrote the first heavy metal tune in my opinion – Helter Skelter! (Jaymz, email, August 2007)

This is interesting because it illustrates the difficulties in trying to define a "typical" audience and the dangers inherent in conflating popular music and youth. The greater visibility of family groups and older fans seems to be linked to the lower cost of tickets for tribute events. Several of those I interviewed said that the price of tickets at stadiums, when added to travel and accommodation costs, made family visits to see original artists prohibitive.[4] Although older fans might be expected to earn more pro-rata than younger music lovers, and could therefore afford higher ticket prices, those I spoke to emphasized that value for money was an important factor in their enjoyment of tributes. With tickets in the region of £8 to £12, an excursion to the local theatre, club or music pub, does not break the bank.

Knowing Me – Knowing You: Getting Close Up and Personal

One of the most striking and enjoyable aspects of the tribute scene its fan-friendly and fan-led ethos. The traditional division between performers and audience is less clear cut, since both could be defined as fans – a sizeable proportion of the musicians are über fans whose love of the music compelled them to perform in the first place. In enacting the role of their chosen icon, performers are able to extend the parameters of their fandom to a level many of us might aspire to yet few will ever reach. However, mindful of the egalitarian nature of the tribute event, they are normally careful not to assume a position of superiority. The challenges of toeing the delicate line between self as (fan) and self as other (star), are exacerbated by the close presence of the audience and the likelihood of an off-stage encounter where role confusion can make meetings slightly awkward. Musicians can't afford to get "too big for their boots" because they must perform in a respectful manner if they are to win the admiration of fans and persuade them to share a little of their affection for the original artist with the tribute.

The difficulties in maintaining traditional fan/star boundaries are magnified in the smaller venues which create an exceptionally fertile environment for the exploration of fantasies. We are accustomed to viewing our favourite stars from a considerable distance at the local mega-stadium where, perched uncomfortably in serried rows, we juggle our drinks, politely containing our emotions and physical responses for fear of upsetting our equally restricted neighbours. In smaller venues where the performers are much more accessible, their adjacency allows the audience to experiment with desires which would normally be restricted to the confines of the imagination. Fans can for example talk to the musicians, touch or flirt with them; shout out song requests in the knowledge that there will be a response; have photographs taken alongside the band and maybe even enjoy the experience of sharing their knowledge and passion on an equal footing over a bottle of beer at the bar. This is empowering, enjoyable, and goes a long way to explaining the popularity of tribute entertainment for those who fail to see the attractions.

For performers too, the experience is distinctive. The closeness of the audience enables musicians to relate to fans at a more personal, individual level, as co-fans with a shared taste in music, or on a fantasy level, through identification with the artist they imitate, as icons, virtuosos and objects of sexual desire. At gigs the complex dynamics can sometimes lead to a degree of role confusion. For the musicians, it is not always clear whether the audience's love and admiration is directed at them or at the artists they represent. As the Bootleg Beatles manager Raj Patel writes, "Regular fans often come to the stage door. We see the same faces at each venue every year. It's hard to fathom sometimes if they are fans of the Bootleg or real Beatles" (Bootleg Beatles, email, March 2009). At Limehouse Lizzy, Dizzy Lizzy and Tizz Lizzy concerts, the audience will chant "Lizzy, Lizzy, Lizzy," when attempting to elicit an encore but which Lizzy do they really want? Is it the archetypal band replete with tragic rock legend Phil Lynott, or is it possible that the audience have developed real love for the substitute? Taking into account Lacan's (1966: 255) observation that "to love is to give what you don't have" – that loving another means recognizing that we are incomplete and, in giving love, we hope to repossess that which we lack – it is probably safe to assume that any Lizzy is better than none – the band are filling an emotional vacuum, whether or not the love expressed is strictly for them.

There is certainly a lot of love in the air. The shared emotional bond with the original artist is often marked by respectful outpourings and references to the archetype from the band. This may involve displaying images of the deceased or defunct, making short speeches regarding their indisputable genius or, in extreme cases, it can even spill over into uncontrollable emotional outbursts. For Geo Fillipedes of US Beatles' tribute Number 9, performance offers mutual opportunities for catharsis and celebration:

> When we did perform for our first benefit back in 2006, the emotions that came over me were overwhelming. I actually had tears in my eyes at some points during the performance and I saw that some of the audience members were equally moved as well. We often share facts and stories about the songs we play and we're finding that our audiences love this aspect of our show. They struck a chord in the hearts and minds of an entire generation in my humble opinion and their memory and music is still going strong. (email, Geo Filippides, February 2009)

In order to win over the audience, arrogance and insincerity must be avoided at all costs – unctuous and emotional gestures are important in establishing sincerity – as they help to offset any suggestion that the band may be capitalizing cynically on the original artist's work.

Once their affection is captured, audiences express their love and dedication in various ways: from very regular attendance at concerts, regardless of location (thus showing commitment beyond the mere call of duty), to posting grateful and flattering comments on band websites. Alternatively, the emotional bond may be cemented via physical contact with the performers – from the foot of the stage, at the bar during the interval, or at the end of the gig when the musicians will sometimes wander informally amongst the audience. These valued encounters provide opportunities to show mutual appreciation as handshakes, hugs, kisses and words of encouragement and gratitude are exchanged. Long-standing tribute acts can develop enduring relationships with individual fans who they look forward to meeting when they make their annual pilgrimage to a particular location. Musicians are equally mindful of the importance of good PR during these encounters and for this reason, regular communication, face-to-face or virtual, is welcomed, as Steven Humphreys of Queen tribute, Mercury, writes:

> We have a guest book on our website where fans can leave comments/reviews and we also put regular band blogs on our news page. We *always* meet fans when asked at venues and are happy to sign tour brochures, etc. Fans send us photos which they take at gigs and we show the good photos on the gallery page. We have regular fans who see us at up to 10 venues each year. (Mercury, email, March 2009)

Clearly, there is an element of "taking care of business" in these fan/performer friendships but I sensed that the musicians, travelling relentlessly up and down the country, really looked forward to seeing some of their "regulars." This was evident in the warmth of the encounters and in the affectionate anecdotes they offered about their fans, even the more "enthusiastic" ones – for at times their love can border on the obsessive.

Loving and Learning to Live with Loss

The Counterfeit Stones have some of the most devoted fans: one couple in particular, Dottie and Dave Prentiss, a pair of 60-somethings have seen their act well over a hundred times. Steve Elson, the band's manager, told me that the senior superfans could usually be spotted on the front row at concerts. In their determination, the Prentiss's exhibit the "excessive enthusiasm" defined by Jenkins (1992: 12) as the hallmark of the true fan, a quality which distinguishes them from the common herd of music lovers. Within the massive arenas where the original Rolling Stones now perform, the couple's fantasies of being noticed would remain unfulfilled, but in Dottie and Dave's case, their devotion was rewarded by The Counterfeits with the privilege of running the band's merchandise stall.

Dottie and Dave's determination to be noticed is relatively benign compared to the antics of the most fanatic fans, whose behaviour borders on downright disturbing. In cases where the original artist's departure has left a significant emotional vacuum, the tribute musician can draw forth on a reservoir of pent-up feelings. For some this affective investment can border on obsession: Veromel and Veromel's (1985) research on fandom uncovered some alarming examples of exaggerated passion, including an extract from a fan letter to David Bowie: "You are the most important thing in my life, the only human being for who [*sic*] I would be able to do sacrifice – you are always in my thoughts and in my soul." Presumably, it is the inaccessibility of the stars which makes them so desirable – if we worked alongside them at the office every day it is unlikely that passions would run so high. Now that Led Zeppelin are, to all intents and purposes inaccessible, their tributes must endure the attentions of obsessive fans who have no other outlet. In an interview before a gig, Whole Lotta Led described one particularly persistent stalker who regularly followed the band. The unnamed female had pursued the group's "Robert Plant" with great tenacity and force, eventually inviting him to stand naked outside a local hotel (he was quick to point out that he did not accept the invitation!).

It is easy to see how tribute bands might play a valuable role in the grieving process. For example, when Marc Bolan's brother Harry Feld first saw T-Rextasy, the shock was so great he was moved to tears at the sight of lead singer Danielz, whose onstage presence so resembles that of his deceased sibling.[5] At a Thin Lizzy tribute event I attended in Bolton, Philomena Lynott, mother of the band's late frontman Phil, seemed deeply touched by the appearance of Tizz Lizzy, a group of Irish teenagers whose lead singer's resemblance to her son is astonishing. To be moved in this way is a natural part of grieving as is a fascination for those who resemble the deceased, but the reaction of the bereaved to the spectral stand-in may be more troubling. Wayne Ellis, describing one of his close encounters with a particularly resolute fan said: "The last girlfriend that Phil [Lynott] had before he died has been plaguing me for a year now. She's obsessed, she turns up at gigs and tries to get hold of my phone number" (Ellis, quoted in Strickland 1995: 15).

At least these people had personal relationships with the fallen idols but what about the rest of us? What is the explanation for our emotional response to the rock and role players? The psychic investment of fans in the love object is explored by Elliot (1999) who sees our obsession with stars and mourning on their passing, as symptomatic of a deeper search for meaning within a culture which fails to provide opportunities for collective mourning, leaving us detached from death and more importantly, from our own mortality. Making contact with our feelings of loss at a tribute event allows us access to the emotional impact of a multitude of other losses, collective as well as personal. Seeing icons such as John Lennon and Jimi Hendrix, portrayed by tribute artists at the height of their careers in all their youthful glory, reminds us not only of the chasm caused by their untimely departure, but the lamentable loss of our own youth, the loss of youthful idealism and the values of an entire generation now gradually heading towards the final curtain. As one reporter at *Time* magazine wrote in response to Lennon's death in 1980, "for much of an entire generation that is passing, as Lennon was, at age 40, into middle age, and coming up against its own mortality – the murder was an assassination, a ritual slaying of something that could hardly be named. Hope perhaps; or idealism. Or time" (Cocks 1980: 22).

In the face of losses, collective as well as personal, the tribute act can provide the audience with a form of spiritual healing because according to Speigel (1990: 193), those who impersonate the famous have the power to act as, "a medium who channels the spirit of a saviour, all the while opening up a public space where people can express their mutual faith in an abstract principle that no one can name." This concept is elaborated by Rosenbaum in his observations on the cult of impersonation surrounding Elvis Presley:

> It's a way of coming to terms with our own sense of loss with what's become of us as a nation – the transition American has made from the young, vital, innocent pioneer national we once were (the young vital Elvis we put on our stamps) to the bloated colossus we well we became: the Fat Elvis of nations.

Although Take That are thankfully, alive and well, having recently regrouped as a "man-band," at a recent Fake That concert, the tribute act unleashed feelings of loss for a member of the audience who recalled the impact of the original boyband on her daughter's life 13 years ago.

> We [Sue and her daughter] came here tonight because she was such a fan back then. I felt such a rush of emotion when the band did some of the old songs and dance routines Milly used to enjoy with her friends when she first went to secondary school. They were all passionate Take That fans who used to descend on our house, declaring their love for the band, reading fan magazines, watching videos together at

> home and screaming their heads off at the concerts I drove them to. It's daft I know but coming here together – it's just reminded me of how it used to be then and the fun we used to have. (Sue, Fake That concert, 2007)

Hearing the music and seeing the dance routines, touched on the loss of Milly's childhood now she had flown the nest and on Sue's role as a mother of young children in a bustling house filled with teenagers.

Music has the capacity to summon up the spectre of our youthful selves, thereby giving us access to the emotions associated with that stage of life. This is because, as Denisoff (1975: 33) explains in a study of the record industry, "A popular music fan is generally wedded to a specific style current in the idiom of his adolescence." For older members of the audience, this enables them to relocate powerful feelings from their youth relating to freedom, love, sexual awakening and friendship. Two middle-aged friends recounted how going together to see a 1960s soul tribute at a Salford nightclub enabled them to access memories of the bond they cemented as teenagers in a small country town.

> We grew up in a place where clubs were pretty limited but we both loved soul music so at weekends, we would go to the local disco above a pub where they played Tamla Motown and Stax records. Our lives totally revolved around music, dancing (and boys of course)! It was like a secret society which only those in the know were aware of. Occasionally we would find someone who had been to one of the bigger clubs in Nottingham or Manchester who knew the latest dance moves. Me and Kate copied them slavishly, dancing together in unison at the disco, showing off our mastery of complex steps, thinking we were impressing everyone. Coming here tonight, the music and dancing brought it all back. It's like we are back at the disco, young, pretty, full of fun – and it reminds us of why we became friends in the first place – we loved soul then and we still love it today. Being here takes us back to being the people we were then and we forget our troubles. If I have had a difficult week at work, I just want to go out and dance. (Kate and Georgie, interview, The Willows Variety Club, November 2007)

In their deliberate use of music to access positive emotional memories, these women show the medium's ability to influence mood, a capacity identified by Wells (1990) who found widespread use of music in the management of feelings. Collective participation at the live event through the re-enactment of youthful identity, transcends the solitary pleasures of private listening by allowing individuals to share their memories publicly.

Collective Participation and Enunciative Productivity

Due to the desire to establish taste hierarchies, critics of live imitative entertainment fail to acknowledge shortcomings in the private consumption of canonized recorded texts and performances and in doing so, they are unable to understand the motivations of fans at tribute events. Turino (2008: 89) attempting to explain the distinction between recorded and participatory music argues that "studio audio art has more in common with sculpture, painting, and other studio art forms than it does with participatory performance." Emphasizing the difference between the forms he goes on to suggest that, "Participatory music *is not simply for listening,*" and moreover, "studio audio art is *not for doing with other people.*"[6] Record ownership is just one element of a much wider process of production and consumption and fan activities clearly extend beyond the boundaries of straightforward musical appreciation. They do not necessarily go to gigs for the sole purpose of seeing a band and listening to music either, since a good deal of their behaviour is rooted in the desire to commune with like-minded others in any manner they chose. For some members of the audience, the music being performed is not particularly relevant and their attention to it is distracted as they go about their evening. The gig provides a social arena where any number of extra-musical activities may take place. I frequently observed people in clubs who spent more time at the bar or chatting at the back of the auditorium and a few who I interviewed claimed that they came to the club on a set night each week regardless of who was performing.

For those who do choose to enjoy the music, the scale of the smaller venues influences the dynamics of performance in ways which alter the character of their experience. The size creates an element of informality which allows for less scripted performance and more opportunities for musicians to use their judgement in determining the character of the gig. While the order of songs may be loosely organized in advance, the proximity of the audience makes it easier to adjust the performance in response to mood, whether by upping the tempo or changing the direction of the music to include more of what the audience appears to want. If the gig is a little flat, the injection of a few up-tempo anthems can instantly lift the spirits. The environment also makes it easier for musicians to read body language or respond to fan requests for particular songs, thereby increasing levels of agency, enjoyment and involvement in the gig. Imitative performers cannot afford the luxury of alienating the audience with the self-indulgence exhibited by certain original artists. Playing all new material and disparaging audience requests for the classic repertoire is strictly verboten, as is deliberately messing around with the delivery of favourite songs. This is a luxury reserved for musical giants like

Bob Dylan and Miles Davis – the crowd will not tolerate such scant disregard for their enjoyment from a tribute.

Enjoyment is also derived from interactions between fans. In the socially motivated setting of the local live gig there are plenty of opportunities for fans to make communal use of texts and practices through "enunciative productivity," a term used by Fiske (1992: 37) to describe the ways in which the individual fan can use shared consumption to interact meaningfully with peers. This activity can take many forms, from showing off T-shirts emblazoned with band logos, singing the lyrics to songs, making recognized hand signals at metal concerts, to filming one another with mobile phones, playing air guitar and "headbanging" in time with the music or, as we have already seen, dancing in any style homologous with the music genre. Knowing the right hand signals and dance moves may seem rather trivial accomplishments, but fans take great pride in displaying the knowledge they have acquired about the object of their fandom since this is a currency which can raise status in the wider fan community. In Fiske's (1992: 43) words "The experts – those who have accumulated the most knowledge – gain prestige within the group ... knowledge, like money, is a source of power."

Fans at the gigs I attended seemed keen to share this knowledge and passion during interviews and the all-consuming nature of their obsession soon became apparent.

> I am 14 and Led Zeppelin are my absolute favourite band of all time even though I never got a chance to see them live. In my opinion music today is just, oh – rubbish and totally lacking in the feeling of rock in the 1960s and 1970s. Most of my friends like hip hop, R&B and dance but I just don't listen to that kind of stuff. I wish more people my age could get into Led Zeppelin – they are just the greatest rock band ever and I will love them forever. In fact, I love them so much, I would seriously consider being buried in a Zeppelin T shirt and I definitely want a Zeppelin tattoo! There are no bad Zeppelin songs and I should know because I must have nearly every one in my collection. It's great that some of the people here feel the same way as me. (Tim, interview, Whole Lotta Led gig, November 2007)

> If you include studio cuts, live releases and a handful of prized bootlegs, I think I have got around 150 songs by Led Zeppelin. Although I enjoy other bands, I really *love* Led Zeppelin and nothing – absolutely nothing anyone says, will ever change my mind! Before I went to secondary school, music wasn't that important to me but in my teenage years I needed something to help me deal with my emotions and Led Zeppelin kept me sane. A big part of who I am is tied up with these

> guys. When I was growing up, they were godlike, mythical figures, someone I wanted to be like – I bought all the posters, T-shirts, DVDs – I drew the ZOSO symbol over all my school books and spent countless hours studying their album covers. I've been married, had a family but I still feel a great affinity with the band and can't see myself ever losing that emotional bond. I come to see Whole Lotta Led because they help me to reconnect with Zeppelin and all those feelings whenever I see them. (Neil, interview, Whole Lotta Led gig, November)

These accounts reveal that the fans measure their commitment to the band through their consumption of records and other material products on offer. In addition, as Hills (2002: x) points out, in purchasing concert tickets, records and CDs, fans are able to use popular culture and the media to construct and perform identities. He develops the concept of "performative consumption" which acknowledges the importance of popular culture and the media in the construction and performance of identity. This means that when fans purchase a concert ticket or CD, the exchange transcends the sphere of economics. These products also enable them to gain the cultural capital they crave and although much of this knowledge is gleaned from the official sources provided by the cultural industries at hugely inflated prices, at tribute events it is possible to augment existing possessions at a fraction of the cost by purchasing T-shirts, programmes and CDs at the merchandise table.

Recognizing the importance attached by fans to the expression of fandom and connoisseurship, tribute performers will provide opportunities to discuss the minor nuances of performance, repertoire and history either face-to-face or virtually. The original bands are served by an official music press which provides a major forum for information about artists and discourses on popular music, establishing who is cool and who is not – upholding the mythological status of certain groups over others. For the tribute bands however, contact with fans must be maintained via alternative media. In the majority of cases this channel of communication is the internet and many of the tribute bands I encountered make use of websites like MySpace to keep in touch with fans. Limehouse Lizzy, for example, has a fiercely loyal collection of fans globally and an international mailing list of over 10,000. Fans enjoy communicating with bands via the websites, offering a running commentary on gigs, sharing their perception of the event, debating the merits of different songs, commenting on the venue, the behaviour of the crowd or anything else relating to their experience of the gig.

Websites are also a powerful forum for the public display of expert knowledge, as exemplified by the following comments posted on band websites:

> Fantastic gig in Sheffield last night! 1st class performance by you all. I keep thinkin' you can't get any better but then everytime I see you, you do! I love you guys! Thanks for keepin' my favourite music alive. See you all again soon x – p.s. ever fancied playin' the slower version of *Don't Believe a Word*, like on *Old Grey Whistle Test* with Moore and Gorham? (Sara from Barnsley, Limehouse Lizzy Guest Book, 13 June 2009)

> Despite having seen the Who many times over the past 29 years (including Charlton '76, the 81 Tour, Tommy at the RFH in '89, Hollywood Bowl 2000, the Forum ×3 last year and others) I'd never seen them perform the mini opera. And I have to say that the band's rendition of *A Quick One While He's Away* (with Pete's edited introduction) was highly entertaining in both its humorous delivery and powerful execution. (Howlin' Pete Wyatt, Who's Who Review Page, Burnham-On-Sea, 7 March 2005)

In both these cases, the writers are drawing attention to their knowledge of the original band's history. The first writer refers to Thin Lizzy's appearance on a cult 1970s televised rock show, where they played a slowed-down version of one of their classic hits, a snippet of information which only a limited number of older fans will probably remember. In the second posting, firstly, the writer reminds readers of his longstanding fan status, thereby positioning himself as an authority. Having established himself as an expert, he goes on to pass judgement on the band's delivery of a particular song the previous evening. The writers' efforts repudiate the mindless consumer stereotype and in doing so, they illustrate Fiske's (1989b) view that fans use popular culture in a purposeful manner, finding opportunities for agency in their consumption of media texts.

Seeing and Being Seen

A striking aspect of the tribute scene is its familiarity, a quality which fans value for, as Fonarow (2006: 207) found, "The gig is an event where the audience wants to believe that the boundaries between music, performer, audience and emotion are effaced." In her study of indie music, she found that fans particularly enjoyed those concerts where bands took the time to mingle in the crowd before or after the shows. The desire for intimacy with performers is by no means genre specific however, and, regardless of what music was played, I found fans delighted in the face-to-face encounters with musicians. Tribute bands capitalize on the fact that original artists are usually remote or unavailable, either dead, defunct, languishing in an expensive private clinic, touring abroad or recording a new album. Even if they were to make an offstage appearance, security issues and the scale of the venue would preclude the possibility of an intimate one-on-one with the megastars. Many of us harbour fantasies about having a live encounter with our favourite performers and some will do almost anything to satisfy their desires. A good deal of the appeal of tributes lies in their accessibility and the fact that the more established bands can be depended upon to make an annual appearance at the friendly local music club or theatre where a chance encounter at the bar and even a relationship, are a real possibility. Add to this the fact that communication via the internet is an additional option, and it is easy to see why tribute acts are so much in demand.

The small-scale gig fulfils a really simple wish to be acknowledged in a culture where so many of us experience alienation. A good deal of the attention-seeking behaviour I observed, could be linked to this fundamental need, as fans employ various strategies in order to achieve just a little personal recognition. In an attempt to be seen, the more determined will set about seeking a position on the front row at seated venues, or directly in front of the stage at standing events. Here, eye contact can be established and by holding arms out towards the stage, physical union may be achieved. From time to time, the musicians respond by reaching into the sea of outstretched hands – touching the lucky few, and at the end of a gig, excitement builds when they mingle with the crowd. Then there are opportunities for the more vocal members of the crowd to draw attention to themselves by making requests for particular songs or directing comments on the performance which can lead to lively banter. This allows the audience to achieve the objective of being seen and heard. The desire to be noticed is not easily extinguished – those who fail to grab any attention in the physical realm of the gig, may take recourse to websites. Messages posted on The Counterfeit Stones website provide some insight into the degree of importance fans attach to being seen. Keen to remind the band of her location in the audience, one fan offers a few personal details by way of an aide-memoire: "hi guys great night at the haslemere hall last night-i was the blonde about four back dancing my head off and waggling my tongue back at you!!!!!!!xxxxxxxxxxx" (Lizzie Marmalade, Counterfeit Stones Guest Book, 5 November 2009). On the same site, another fan attempts to draw attention to herself.

> We had a fabulous time (again) in Tunbridge Wells on 22 May. But was disappointed you didn't sing about me this time – you started a show in Maidstone a while back singing about me and I was well impressed. They couldn't do a thing with me all evening after that!... Good luck for future gigs and will see you next time around. Don't know why you don't come to Hastings though – we do have a theatre you would pack to the rafters and the fish 'n' chips are good ... luv you all. (Oh Carol, Counterfeits Stones Guestbook, 4 June 2009)

Although disappointed by the recent snub, the writer was clearly delighted that the band had at least acknowledged her on a previous occasion. Her attempts to lure the band to Hastings, are indicative of the desire for agency and control over the object of fandom identified by Elliot (1999: 110). In a similar message, a fan relives momentary recognition and then attempts to forge intimacy with Limehouse Lizzy by referring to what he assumes are mutually remembered experiences of an annual rock event held on the Greek island of Rhodes:

> Hey lads, yes its that scouse fella who wouldn't shut up because he was so happy that he had the chance to say thanx ... thanx for a great gig, for making my birthday, for talking to me through the blur ... you are just the best dudes and I will never forget those Rhodes moments ... keep it live and be safe always, see you soon, Colin. (Colin, Limehouse Lizzy Guest Book, 25 June 2009)

Postings like these show how much fans crave validation. Although the artists are clearly seeking admiration, respect and love from the audience, whether during performance when they may be playing in character, or offstage when they resort to their everyday identity, fans are equally keen to be identified by the performers. In an epoch characterized by alienation and purposelessness, tribute musicians by assuming a celebrity identity, are invested with the magical power of the famous to make individuals feel less insignificant. Favourable acknowledgement from the star can add a meaningful dimension to life and the humble endeavours of fans – it is heartening to observe the pleasure derived from these encounters.

The postings on websites reveal that the relationship between the tribute musicians and their audience is in many ways similar to that of the traditional fan/performer dyad where the fan feels and expresses love and admiration for the inaccessible star. However, the relationship is unstable because although tribute performers are invested with power from the star identity they inhabit, this is only because the audience give them permission to occupy that role. In this sense the artist/audience relationship is characterized by a shifting equilibrium where participants change places depending on the role they currently occupy. A tribute artist can lose celebrity status offstage and the lack of aura can cause the fan/star relationship to evaporate.

An effective performance requires that audience and artist collude in believing the identity enacted onstage. Both Dyer (1979) and Vermorel and Vermorel (1985) observed a concern for qualities of authenticity amongst fans and for this reason a credible front has to be maintained. However, whilst performing the music and identity of another, those engaged in paying tribute may be acting in ways which are contrary to their everyday identity but the performance does not necessarily end when they leave the stage. Like professional actors and the social actors described by Goffman (1959) in his dramaturgical analysis of human interaction, they are confronted with the problem of deciding whether or not to maintain their performative identity at all times. Musicians may experience difficulties in relating to fans as they resume their everyday identities – in relinquishing the star identity any ego-enhancement endowed by the borrowed signifiers may be lost. Fans must also make a rapid transition from relating to the fantasy figure and speak instead, to the ordinary individual who only 5 minutes earlier appeared to be a star. It may be a disappointment to discover that the person standing before you in the bar who only a few minutes before, looked and sounded so like Bono, is not at all inspiring and would probably struggle to string together a limerick, let alone a memorable power-ballad.

If on the other hand, the performer is able to maintain and incorporate elements of the mysterious star aura into their own identity, it is difficult not to keep relating to them as a star-stricken fan. My own perception of performers off-stage was tinged with a complex mixture of awe and disappointment – the more committed, convincing and gifted the performer, the greater the frisson of excitement on meeting them face-to-face and yet disappointment quickly took over when any discrepancies between star and everyday identity surfaced. The arrogant figure strutting about the stage, commanding the audience with every fibre of their body, could be unprepossessing, mundane even, when out of character. A sexy mid-Atlantic onstage accent could easily revert to the reviled strains of broadest "Brummie" in offstage moments.[7] Although it was clear that they were not really the people they were imitating and we both knew this, I wondered how I could have been so easily duped in the first place – but then as Evans (2005: 1) reminds us, stardom is not the result of innate, magnetic qualities – celebrity status is constructed by the press, television, film and video. By inhabiting the pre-constructed persona, tribute artists illustrate the media's extraordinary ability to create identities and our willingness to project our feelings of love and admiration onto the faux celebrities, shows the extent to which we are happy to collude if it allows us to commune with the stars. Deep-down, we know that they are not really any different to ourselves but we still choose to legitimize their A-list status. We allow tribute artists to inhabit the celebrity space even if their resemblance to the original is tangential or fleeting because the imagination is able to transcend any physical discrepancies to allow us to experience the star/fan relationship. Like the stars which they represent, tribute performers are much more than a simple by-product of capitalism. As Dyer explains, stars function as a social phenomenon, generated by fans for their own purposes because:

> [They] represent typical ways of behaving, feeling and thinking in contemporary society, ways that have been socially, historically and culturally constructed ... Stars are also the embodiments of the social categories in which people are placed and through which they make sense of their lives, and indeed through which we make our lives. (Dyer, 1987)

Case Study – Limehouse Lizzy concert Manchester Academy 1, 13 October 2007

Despite the fact that the band faced competition at Academies 2 and 3 from Mark Ronson, cult indie band Puressence and American singer songwriter Mary Gauthier a sizeable audience turned up at the venue. Of the 500 strong crowd around two-thirds were well below the age of 40 and a small subgroup bunched in front of the stage consisted of minors aged 9–13 who had come along with relatives. Twenty-one-year-old student Mark said he had been introduced to the band by his father and that he had dragged Frankie, his girlfriend along, to keep him company. She admitted that she had not been a fan of the band but added that she had really enjoyed the evening and would like to come to another similar gig. A group of three 30-somethings confessed that they were deeply interested in the music of Thin Lizzy and had come along with a view to improving their own performance as musicians in a local band. They had become familiar with the original music through listening to albums and they saw the event as one of the best ways to celebrate and keep alive the "timeless classics" of the 1970s. Since their own band's live set featured some Thin Lizzy covers, this was an ideal opportunity to listen and learn in order to inform their own playing. The crowd, who didn't necessarily grow up to the sounds of Lynott and co. in their original context appeared to be familiar with the majority of the lyrics and at times, when invited to by the band, were more than happy to shout them out. As the evening wore on, a number of male fans strummed air guitars excitedly and male and female members of the crowd began to shake their hair with wild abandonment, rocking backwards and forwards, resting only occasionally to recharge their batteries or regain their balance. The children and some of the students at the foot of the stage frequently raised their hands up in an attempt to touch the guitarists who, from time to time, acquiesced to the plea for physical union. At the end of the final set, the band walked off to screams for "Lizzy," "Lizzy" returning less than reluctantly with the offer of a choice of songs and for several minutes, a ferocious battle raged between those who wanted *Black Rose* and the rest who preferred *Whiskey in the Jar*. As Limehouse played both, neither party went home dissatisfied and at the end of the evening the satisfied and exhausted crowd wound their way around the carpet of plastic glasses and out into the mild autumn night.

Notes

1. Introduction

1. Tom Cox, "Clonin' Jack Flash," *The Guardian*, 3 April, 2005.
2. B. Viner, "Brentwood, vould you like to dance?," *The Independent*, 18 December, 2000. The article goes on to explain that the band, one of the 40 Abba tributes currently available for hire in the England, has two line-ups playing simultaneously in the UK and abroad.
3. Culshaw (2004) discusses the Bootleg Beatles' performance of the song "A Day in the Life," a composition seen by many to be a quintessential moment in 1960s popular music due to its innovative production techniques and complex arrangements. The cacophonous orchestra crescendo made it a particularly ambitious and groundbreaking work and live performance of this song is particularly challenging.
4. This story was the inspiration behind the Wahlburg's (2001) film *Rock Star* where copier repairman Chris Cole, whose fanaticism about heavy metal band Steel Dragon eventually leads to him being taken on to replace sacked lead singer Bobby Beers.
5. Jon Pareles, "Brad Delp, 55, Lead Singer for Boston, Dies," *The New York Times*, 10 March 2007. (Boston's eponymous debut album, recorded in Delp's basement, sold 17 million copies and was one of the best-selling debut albums in American history.)
6. SingStar and Guitar Hero are registered trademarks for competitive music games designed to be played on home computers.
7. Described by the BBC as the "morose centrepiece of the album," "Some Will Pay (For What Others Pay To Avoid)," was the title of a track on Devoto's 1983 album *Jerky Visions of the Dream* (Virgin UK).
8. T-Rextasy have composed, recorded and performed music in the style of the original T Rex. Their lead singer Danielz told me the band have even completed some of Marc Bolan's unfinished work. Pink Floyd tribute The Machine were praised by *Rolling Stone* for the improvisations they add to their reinterpretations of the original Floyd sound. (See Daniel Kreps "All Fillers, no Killers: a Novice's Guide to Tribute Bands," *Rolling Stone*, 13 February, 2007.)

2. Tribute Bands in Context

1. With worldwide sales of over 26 million the album, *ABBA Gold* (a compilation initially released after PolyGram acquired the rights to the band's back catalogue), illustrates the benefits to be gained from recycling existing material. One source rates it as the 39th best selling album of all time <http://www.mediatraffic.de/alltime-album-chart.htm>.

2. See: "Exoticism and Nostalgia London's Bohemia 1967–1973," <www.vam.ac.uk/collections/fashion/features/1960s/exhibition/exoticism_nostalgia/index.html>.
3. Manchester Music Tours invites visitors on a general pilgrimage around the musical landmarks in order that they can see for themselves "the sights of the city that inspired the Manchester music scene." For the specialist, there are further opportunities to take separate Oasis, Smiths' or Joy Division tours, <www.manchestermusictours.com>.
4. <www.mathewstreetfestival.com>.
5. <www.vibeforphilo.com>.
6. Emma Henry and Natalie Paris, "Lez, not Led, Zeppelin to play Bonnaroo in US," *The Daily Telegraph*, 8 February, 2008.
7. From modest beginnings where the event made a loss, it is now described as "Europe's Biggest Tribute Band Music Festival." Last year's programme included tributes to Amy Winehouse, Led Zeppelin, the Sex Pistols, Oasis and the Kaiser Chiefs. Tickets for the festival were on sale for the modest price of £47.50 for three days <www.glastonbudget.co.uk>.
8. Following his exposure as a forger, Keating was eventually awarded sufficient stature to present a television programme on the techniques of the old masters whose work he had so capably imitated. See Mark Jones (ed.), *Fake? The Art of Deception*. London: British Museum Publications, 1990.
9. The study identifies a close knit community of traders operating in the Notting Hill, Portobello and Ladbroke Grove area of London and similar development on a smaller scale around Covent Garden and Greenwich. In the north of England, the shopping complex Affleck's Palace in Manchester provides a focal point for provincial second-hand retailing.
10. See Tim Hyland, "Clothier on magical mystery tour replicating Beatles suits," *Baltimore Business Journal*, 11 April 2008. According to Hyland, the business decision was based on Lease's observation that while, "Every city has 1,000 Elvis impersonators ... I don't think people realize how many Beatles tribute bands are out there."
11. See Beatles' tribute, 1964 The Tribute, re-enacting the event at <www.youtube.com/watch?v=flRVz1FH2WU>.
12. For example, the final takings of the Rolling Stones' 2005, "A Bigger Bang" tour reached $558,255,524. It is estimated that 4,680,000 people attended the 144 shows, making it the highest grossing tour in history. Ray Waddell, "Rolling Stones Tour Grosses More Than Half A Billion," *Billboard*, 3 October, 2007.
13. According to Brian May, Queen's *We will Rock You* was specifically written for the large scale stadium to allow the audience to feel at one with the band. (Source, "We Are the Champions: Stadium Rock 1965–1993," *Seven Ages of Rock*, BBC 2, May 2007.)

3. From "Ghost" and Cover Bands, to Pop Parody and Tributes

1. *Collins Essential English Dictionary*, 2nd Edition. London: HarperCollins, 2006.
2. For a discussion on the posthumous performance, read the BBC news feature: "Singing from beyond the grave" <http://news.bbc.co.uk/go/pr/fr/-/1/hi/entertainment/8299647.stm> (accessed 12 October 2009).
3. Jonathan Thompson, "At last – the list to end all lists A bluffer's guide through the blizzard of Millennium polls," *The Independent*, 28 November 1999.

4. Alan Riding, "Arts Abroad: Rock and the Queen to Celebrate Each Other," *The New York Times*, 30 May 2002.
5. The event at the Lincoln memorial featured performances from distinguished artists such as Beyonce Knowles, Mary J Blige, Herbie Hancock, Bruce Springsteen, Stevie Wonder and Sheryl Crow. Jon Pareles discusses the role of music in communicating inclusivity in "Lyrical Messages About an Inclusive America," *New York Times*, 18 January 2009.
6. Examples of this popular format include: *The Hundred Greatest Albums* (Channel 4) and VH1 programmes, *The 100 Greatest Songs of the '80s* and *The 100 Greatest One Hit Wonders.*
7. Frith's point is illustrated in an example of televisual homage from the 1960s. In *The Dusty Show*, British pop singer Lulu celebrates the work of contemporary vocal artist, Dusty Springfield. The deferential, conformist tone of the programme corresponds to adult, rather than youth audience expectations. The effect of this, is a dilution of the raw power and intensity of Springfield's music.
8. Despite monumental success as a performer and recording star, Elvis Presley's credibility as an artist was somewhat compromised by the fact that he did not write his own material. This is because the ability to compose and play original music is valued more highly than the embodiment and performance of that music.
9. This indicates that record buying is one of the few areas of consumption where price is not a determining factor in product differentiation. Martin (2009) provides a discussion about the relative merits of Embassy records in, John Martin, "Embassy Records, Embassy Label Cover Versions from Woollies. Good or Bad?" <www.embassyrecords.co.uk/> (accessed 1 May 2009).
10. For information about the Mozart Festival Orchestra, see <www.raymondgubbay.co.uk>.
11. For example, Tex Beneke, the signature saxophone, soloist and singer with the original Glen Miller Band, who went on to lead a Miller ghost band. Only a few of the ghost bands currently play full time – The Glen Miller Orchestra being one. As they are such large scale enterprises, bands will tour only if enough bookings are lined up to make their appearance financially viable. For general information about ghost bands, visit Christopher Popa's Big Band Library website: <www.bigbandlibrary.com>.
12. Washington, a black American, fronted the white British band on *Hand Clappin' Foot Stompin' Funky-Butt ... Live!* (1966) and *Hipsters, Flipsters, Finger-Poppin' Daddies!* (1967). The success of the Rolling Stone's record, *Got Live if You Want It*, also reflects the popularity of live music and covers at this time. Released in the UK during 1965, all six of the EP's tracks, are cover versions of American R&B hits.
13. Live music's popularity may have diminished with the rise of the disco but it continued to play an important role in informing judgements of value and authenticity concerning popular music. During the 1960s arguments on the subject of live performance as a measure of credibility, dominated the music press – *The New Musical Express* devotes a good deal of space to debates about contemporary musicians' live competence See, for example: C. Hutchins, *New Musical Express*, 26 February 1965.
14. In 1970 there were around 250 professional Elvis impersonators whereas today, conservative estimates point to around 35,000. If this trend continues at the same rate, by 2060, there could be millions of Elvis impersonators worldwide <www.elvis.net>.

15. In the song, the Dave Clark Five song *Bits and Pieces* became *Boots and Blisters. Call Up The Groups* reached the number three position in the UK in 1964 and remained in the charts for 13 weeks (*Guinness Book of British Hit Singles* [2000], p. 91). The band website gives further information about their parody records of the 1960s. See: <http://www.barronknights.com/>.
16. According to Brian May, Queen's *We will Rock You* was specifically written for the large scale stadium to allow the audience to feel at one with the band. BBC 2 "We Are the Champions: Stadium Rock 1965–1993," *Seven Ages of Rock* (May 2007).
17. The 1994 album, *Michael White Plays the Music of Led Zeppelin* (Griffin Records) was awarded seven out of a possible ten marks in *The Collectors Guide to Heavy Metal* (Popoff 1997). *Metal*, Burlington: Collectors Guide Publishing.
18. Dave Lewis (2003) *Tight But Loose Files: Celebration II* (London: Omnibus), p. 49.
19. The importance of rock photography is sometimes overlooked in music histories. Neal Preston, a high profile rock photographer, worked with many top artists including Queen, Bruce Springsteen and The Who, and was also Led Zeppelin's tour photographer during the 1970s.

4. Establishing a Typology

1. From a review of the 2009 Abbey Road on the River festival held in Louisville, Kentucky.
2. Alongside the more typical Abba, Queen and Madonna acts, Yorkshire based company Tribute-Entertainment advertises tributes to the Blues Brothers and James Bond <http://www.tribute-entertainment.co.uk>.
3. For images of the band in action taken by rock photographer Toni Wells at LA club, Mr. T's Bowl, see <http://www.toniwells.com/b_nudistpriest.htm> (accessed 3 March 2005). For information about Mandonna, Richard Cheese and Tragedy, go to the following websites: <www.mandonna.com> and <www.myspace.com/letsmaketragedyhappen>, <www.richardcheese.com>.
4. See J. Rice and D. Roberts (eds), *Guinness Book of British Hit Singles* (13th Edition) (London: Guinness World Records Ltd., 2000). Some measure of Richard's popularity can be gathered from the fact that, like Elvis Presley, he is one of the few artists to have hit records in the charts during five consecutive decades.
5. Doss (1999: 158) suggests that there were already something in the region of 20,000 Elvis impersonators in the late 1990s, a figure which has undoubtedly multiplied alarmingly in the meantime.
6. According to Nic Fleming (2007) a study of over 1,000 famous musicians found that they were nearly twice as likely to die earlier than the general population. Deaths were mainly due to drug and alcohol abuse.
7. Fury's entry which places him at position 36 in the book's Top 500 says that he: "Scored more hits in the 1960s than fellow Liverpudlians The Beatles and spent 291 weeks on chart." Unlike The Beatles though, he failed to reach the number one slot. Dansatak Entertainment Agency offer Rob Dee and the Fury Sound <http://www.dansatak.com/>. See also: The Fury Sound: a Tribute to Billy Fury <http://www.billyfurytribute.com/> and The Sound of Fury <http://www.thesoundoffury.co.uk/>.

8. Richard Williams, "Performance: ABBA – Albert Hall," *The Sunday Times*, 15 February 1977, p. 9.
9. Due to family commitments, the band had to limit their travelling and videos were used in place of personal appearances to placate their international fans. ABBA made more use of video than many of their contemporaries in a period when its use as promotional tool was still in its infancy. Their brightly colour co-ordinated costumes and dance sequences, combined with close ups of the two ABBA girls, created an unforgettable and unique vision of 1970s chic.
10. Perhaps the most bizarre examples, No Kill I, a Sacramento punk Band, are one of several musical tributes to the television series *Star Trek* <http://www.nokilli.com/>.
11. For a review of the event see: Abe Bayer, "Rain Men: World's Pre-eminent Beatles tribute band revisits Seattle," *Journal Newspapers*, 21 April 2004 <www.zwire.com> (accessed 13 November 2008).
12. Impressario Howes was one of Britain's leading promoters whose clients included leading pop groups of the day including The Beatles.
13. Redlands was the Sussex home of Keith Richards which was raided in 1967 by the drugs squad after a tip-off by the tabloid press. The incident led to a media furore and although Jagger and Richards were both charged and sentenced, following an appeal they were offered a conditional discharge. The Rolling Stones made an appearance on *Jukebox Jury*, the British television panel pop programme in July 1964, disrupting rehearsals to such an extent that the live show almost didn't go to air <http://www.nostalgiacentral.com/tv/variety/jukeboxjury.htm>.
14. Davis' use of the term "reverence bands" correlates with the term "sound-alike" which I use in preference. See the article, Davis, Giles "Identity Theft – Tribute Bands, Grand Rights, and Dramatico-Musical Performances," *Cardozo Arts and Entertainment Law Journal* 24 (November 2006): 845, for a discussion of the distinctions between the two.
15. See their websites: <http://www.nearlydan.co.uk/> and <http://stealingdan.co.uk/main.htm>.
16. Alive Network website <http://www.alivenetwork.com/bandsearch.asp?style=Tribute%20bands>.
17. T. Halpin, "Vladimir Putin flies in Bjorn Again for Abba tribute concert," *The Times*, 6 February 2009.
18. See <http://www.wholelottaled.co.uk/> (accessed 13 July 2007).
19. Newcastle based tribute, The Benwell Floyd shows that they adopt a similar stance, YouTube performances show them focusing their attention on careful reproduction of the sound rather than looks. Bennett (2000: 171) provides a more detailed discussion of their work.
20. Charlotte Heathcote discusses the work of Whole Lotta Led in "Led Astray: Can any tribute band match Led Zeppelin's legendary excess?," *Sunday Express*, 2 December 2007, p. 59.
21. The Rock and Roll Hall of Fame's, "500 Songs that Shaped Rock and Roll" <http://www.rockhall.com/exhibithighlights/500-songs/>.
22. Moe Meyer's uses this phrase in an analysis of techniques used in the New York, Women's One World avant garde performance space where alternative female sexualities are enacted for an assumed lesbian audience.

23. Band Websites: <www.acdshe.com/>, <www.hellsbelles.info/>, <www.theironmaidens.com/>, www.lezzeppelin.com/>.
24. The homosocial bond, especially that between male songwriting and performing duos, often exhibits all the hallmarks of a passionate love affair – witnessed in the very public fallings out of Mick Jagger and Keith Richards; John Lennon and Paul McCartney – all of whom have been famous for their major feuds as much as they are for their songwriting ability. This theme is exploited fully in the film *Some Kind of Monster* (2004) which analyses the intensity of the homosocial bond between Lars Ulrich and James Hetfield of Metallica and the fiery energy underpinning the band's creative force.
25. In their study of the relationship between a gay lifestyle, musical taste and cultural preference, the disco genre was described by Woods and Franks (2006: 158) as "the true siren song of the gay lib era."
26. For the Duke of Uke, see <http://home.pacifier.com/~jimcser/> (accessed 3 October 2008). For Schlong, go to <http://www.allmusic.com/cg/amg.dll?p=amg&sql=10:3ifoxqljldfe> (accessed 3 October 2008).
27. The band's album *Sabbatum*, promises to take listeners on a temporal voyage to enjoy the truly unique experience of a Black Sabbath show held in the fourteenth century where, they can enjoy listening to the thunderous strains of *War Pigs* and *The Wizard* played on lute and the harp <http://www.rondellus.ee/html/record.html>.
28. See *New Musical Express*, 4 July 2001, pp. 12–13.
29. Maddy Costa describes Li'l G'n'R in "Welcome to the Jungle," *The Guardian*, 17 March 2004. See a video of a battle of the bands between Li'l G'n'R and Tiny Motley Crue at the band's website: <www.lilgnr.net>.

5. Getting Established and Maintaining a Career

1. On the 10 December 2007, 28 years after they last played a full set together, Led Zeppelin played to a packed house at the O2 Arena in London. Over one million people took part in a ballot for 9,000 pairs of tickets made available.
2. The "Never Ending Tour" is the term used to describe Bob Dylan's relentless, post-1988 performing schedule. Dylan's impressive total of 99 gigs in 2006 compares unfavourably with the average 200 plus of the top tributes.
3. Although professional management is available, the majority of the bands I encountered operate as small businesses, employing less than ten people.
4. The 2009 UCAS website lists 20 UK universities offering named two and three year degree programmes in Popular Music and many other higher education providers now offer courses in music production and performance. At City College in Manchester, the diploma is taught by staff who are, almost exclusively, practising professionals from the recording, performing and management sectors of the North West music industry. Their students who wish to pursue a career as performers study the following specialist units: Music Performance Techniques; Music Performance Session Styles; Working and Developing as a Musical Ensemble; Improvisation; Aural Perception; Music Sequencing; Functional Music Keyboard; Specialist Subject Investigation; Composing and Arranging and Studio Recording Techniques.

5. Kevin Braddock, "Fame Academy: The Brit School," *The Independent*, 28 January 2007.
6. Although rivalry is fierce, musicians recognize the need for co-operation. For example, Wayne Ellis of Limehouse Lizzy told me that during a period of illness, his lead vocal/bass player role was covered by his counterpart from a rival Thin Lizzy tribute act.
7. See Everett's (2001) account of The Beatles' musical apprenticeship which describes their use of other artists' material.
8. This needs to be seen in the context of the research findings of Finnegan (1989) and Cohen (1991) which suggest that there is approximately one band per thousand people (Negus 1999: 41).
9. A growing number of tributes have moved into merchandising, selling anything from T shirts to CDs and posters, but I was unable to establish how much income this aspect of their work generated.
10. Danielz' experience illustrates the blurring of the boundaries between imitative and original musicians. Like many of those on the tribute scene, he has worked with many high-profile artists including Cedric Sharpley, Lindsey Bridgewater and Paul King (a founder member of 1970s folk/rock group Mungo Jerry. More information about the band's history and achievements can be found at Danielz' home page: <www.danielz.co.uk>.
11. Australian rock band The Baby Animals released their first album in 1991. It spent six weeks at number one and was, at the time, the highest selling debut album in Australian rock history.
12. Visit the Counterfeit Stones website at: <www.thecounterfeitstones.net>.
13. <www.stereotonics.co.uk/>.
14. *My Life With Morrissey*, 2003 (dir. Andrew Overtoom).
15. Nathan's likeness has helped the band to achieve considerable success as Sex Pistols doubles in several documentaries – *Blood on the Turntables*, BBC 3, 2004, *Death By Excess*, Sky, 2006 and *God Save the Sex Pistols*, Sky, 2006.
16. Limehouse Lizzy's critical acclaim remains unchallenged. They were voted Band of the Year by *Guitar Magazine* in 2001 and *Loaded* magazine described them as the "best tribute band in the world." The ultimate accolade was conferred on Limehouse when members Andy Fox and Wayne Ellis were invited by Thin Lizzy's guitarists Brian Robertson to join his band, The Clan. See: Andy Strickland, "The Boys Really Are Back in Town," *Loaded* (October 1995).
17. Official tables charting the popularity of tribute acts are hard to come by, The UK Performing Rights Society's top ten league table indicates that the pop genre predominates over rock. This finding reinforces Dave Hickey's (1997: 15) observation that while 90 percent of popular songs are love songs, "ninety percent of rock criticism [is] about the other ten percent."
18. "Tribute band lookalikes go cutting edge," Reuters, 31 May 2007.
19. There are for example, at least four tributes whose choice of the name Hollywood Rose refers to earlier incarnation of Guns and Roses: Hollywood Rose (Italy), while Hollywood Rose (Hungary), Hollywood Rose (Canada) and Hollywood Roses (California).

20. On The Beatles Tribute Band website, West Country mop-tops, The Torquay Beatles, offer "a fully self-contained show including disco" charge £1,500 for two 40–45 minute sets on weekends and evenings <http://www.beatles-tribute-band-uk.co.uk/>.

6. The Value of Paying Tribute

1. For example in Kris Curry and Rich Fox's "rockumentary" *Tribute* (2001) USA, Tribute Films, a study of the careers of six bands, which was referred to in *Film Comment* as: "a bottomless quagmire of melodramatic weirdness." Stephen Herek's quasi-fictional film *Rock Star* (2001) USA, Warner Brothers, following the rock and roll life of the fictional heavy metal band Steel Dragon who recruit a replacement singer from the ranks of the local tribute scene, treads the well-worn path of *Spinal Tap* with its heavy-handed emphasis on parody. In a similar vein, Nicola Robert's BBC2 documentary film *Into the Limelight* (2007) is tinged with pathos and low-key humour as it explores the working lives of tribute artists performing at a small live music venue in the north of England.
2. See Anne Sheppard (1987: 5–7) for a comprehensive overview of Plato's thoughts on the subject of art as imitation as elaborated in *The Republic.* His views are important since they have played a major role in informing cultural criticism, particularly regarding the nature of representation within the arts.
3. Where they are described by German novelist Richter as "so heissen sie Leute die sie selbst sehen" or "so people who see themselves are called."
4. Paul McCartney can play left-handed guitar (with the strings in the correct order) or right-handed guitars adjusted for left-handed playing. *Taxman*, written by George Harrison, was the opening track on The Beatles' *Revolver* album of 1966. Although Harrison wrote the song, the guitar solo was played by Paul McCartney. *Guitar* magazine (November 1987), contains an analysis of the song. For fan comments on The Bootleg Beatles' version of *Taxman*, go to <www.youtube.com/watch?v=P0vNrD-pHIk>.
5. There is a discussion about Gropius's opening speech at the Bauhuas in Ulrich Conrad's (1975) *Programs and Manifestoes on 20thC Architecture* (Cambridge: MIT Press), p. 49.
6. *"Arena" Into the Limelight* (BBC 2007). Directed by Nicola Roberts.
7. According to Mundy (1999: 90) "An examination of the most popular performers on record between 1948 and 1955 reveals a limited rota of artists, mainly white but some black, whose names dominate over and over again." These include the Andrews Sisters, the Mills Brothers, Frank Sinatra, Doris Day and the phenomenally successful Bing Crosby, described by Negus (2001: 24) as "the first modern star to be created via the connection between records, radio and film."
8. Phyllis Stark (1994: 4) discusses the importance of *Billboard* in league tables of song popularity during the 1930s and 1940s.
9. *Sh-Boom* by the Crew Cuts was a typical example of this kind of cover. According to Belz (1990: 26) the record was released by the Chords in 1954 and soon hit the charts as a best seller, eventually reaching the top ten. The popularity of the song can be measured by the number of covers versions made, starting with the Crew Cuts

rendition (which also made it into the top ten). Other covers soon followed, including one by Sy Oliver (Bell Records) another by Billy Williams (Coral Records) and Bobby Williamson created a country version.

10. In a leader article (22 November 1966), p. 1. *Rolling Stone* argues that the commercial standards of showbusiness, "a group of media based on artifice, deception or unreality" should not be applied to rock which "stood for exactly the opposite."
11. 17 USC, Section 102.
12. For a discussion about the case see Owen Bowcott, "A Whiter Shade of Pale: House of Lords asked to rule in copyright wrangle," *The Guardian*, 22 April 2009.
13. See for example: Neuberger (1924), Kurz (1948), Isnard (1960), Savage (1963), Dutton (1983). Following an exhibition on fakes held at the British Museum the book *Fake? The Art of Deception* (ed. Mark Jones) was published in 1990.
14. As a member of The Yardbirds and Cream in the early 1990s, and finally as a solo artist in 2000 <www.rockhall.com/inductee/eric-clapton>.
15. In the following review of the Album *Layla and Other Assorted Love Songs*, from which the track was taken, Allman's creative input is clearly acknowledged. "Clapton leads a crackerjack group, with standout slide guitarist Duane Allman, creating one of the greatest collaborations ever recorded, the two musicians prodding each other to mystical heights. Pain drips from the groove of this seminal record that has something for everyone – hard-driving rockers, stormy blues, wailing solos, including 'Layla' as it was meant to be sung, with the most stunning opening riff written by Eric for his secret love Patti Boyd, then married to his best pal George Harrison." *Zagat Survey Music Guide – 1,000 Top Albums of All Time* (New York: Zagatsurvey, 2003).
16. Many stars die young – Bellis (2007), reveals that for rock and pop stars, the average age of death was 42 years for North American stars and 35 for European with the majority dying within only a few years of achieving fame. Whilst those who die young are usually remembered with a fixed identity, those who go on to sustain a lengthy career, whether due to deliberate reinvention or changing musical direction, may negotiate a series of changing identities.
17. Sadly, he was unable to accept due to health problems! See Douglas Noble, "Australian Pink Floyd Workshop," *Guitar & Bass Magazine* (January 2004).
18. <http://www.drawtheline.net>.
19. <www.kissonline.com>.
20. *Midler v. Ford Motor Co.*, 849 F. 2d 1395 (9th Cir. 1992).
21. *Apple Corps Ltd. v. Leber et al.*, 229 U.S.P.Q. 1015 (1986).
22. Ibid. (1016).
23. See "A Madness tribute band has been asked to pay £500 for copying the original band's famous walk," <http://news.bbc.co.uk/1/hi/england/hereford/worcs/3182025.stm>.
24. *The Dialogues of Plato*, 3rd edn, Vol. 1, *Ion*, trans. B. Jowett. Oxford: Oxford University Press, 1951, p. 533.

7. Fandom and Collective Participation

1. See Joli Jenson (1992), "Fandom as pathology: the consequences of characterization," in L .A. Lewis, (ed.), *The Adoring Audience*. London: Routledge.

2. The song *Tutti Frutti* contained the following lines "A wop bop a loo mop, a good goddam! / Tutti frutti, loose booty / If it don't fit, don't force it / You can grease it, make it easy." It was rewritten in the studio by Dorothy LaBosterie. See Jonathan Buckley (ed.), *The Rough Guide to Rock*. London: Rough Guides Ltd., 2003, p. 603.
3. Tribfest and Glastonbudget are annual cut-price music festivals held in East Yorkshire and Leicestershire. For further information go to the festival websites: <www.tribfest.co.uk> and <www.glastonbudget.net>.
4. The cost of tickets (including camping), for a family of two adults and two teenage children at the Glastonbudget festival was £165.50 in 2009. At the official Glastonbury 2010 festival, a similar sized group would need to pay around £740.
5. Feld's reaction to T-Rextasy is described by Cox (2002).
6. Original author's italics.
7. Despite the fact that regional accents are more acceptable than they once were, a recent study found that those who speak with the distinctive nasal tones of the Birmingham region are seen as much less intelligent than those with other accents. Research carried out by Bath Spa University revealed that the Birmingham accent was deemed as "worse than silence" (Bennett 2008).

Bibliography

Adorno, Theodor. 2001 [1941]. "On Popular Music." In *Understanding Popular Music*, Roy Shuker, p. 19. London: Routledge.

Amanda Andrew. 2009. "Live music helps us beat the doom and gloom." *The Daily Telegraph*, 26 March.

Barnes, Jonathan, ed. 1999. *The Complete Works of Aristotle*. Princeton, NJ: Princeton.

Baudrillard, Jean. 1981. *For a Critique of the Political Economy of the Sign*. St Louis, MO: Telos.

— 1983. *Simulacra and Simuaition*. New York: Semiotexte.

— 1994. *Simulacra and Simulation*, Ann Arbor, MI: University of Michigan Press.

Bayton, Mavis. 1998. *Frock Rock: Women Performing Rock Music*. Oxford: Oxford University Press.

Bellis, Mark, Tom Hennell, Clare Lushey, Karen Hughes, Karen Tocque and John R. Ashton. 2007. "Elvis to Eminem: quantifying the price of fame through early mortality of European and North American Rock and Pop Stars." *Journal of Epidemiology and Community Health* 61: 896–901.

Beltz, Carl. 1969. *The Story of Rock*. New York: Oxford University Press.

— 1970. *The Story of Rock*. New York: Oxford University Press.

Benjamin, Walter. 1973. "The work of art in an age of mechanical reproduction." In *Illuminations*, pp. 211–44. London: Fontana Press.

Bennett, Andy. 2000. *Popular Music and Youth Culture*. Basingstoke: Palgrave Macmillan.

Bennett, Andy. 2001. *Cultures of Popular Music*. Buckingham: Open University Press.

Bennett, H. Stith. 1980. *On Becoming a Rock Musician*. Amherst, MA: University of Massachusetts Press.

Bennett, Rosemary. 2008. "Brummie accent is perceived as 'worse than silence'." *The Times*, 4 April.

Blakemore, Helena. 1990. 'Acid – Burning A Hole In The Present'. In *Readings In Popular Culture*, ed. Gary Day, pp. 18–22. New York: St Martin's Press.

Booth, Michael, and Joel Kaplan. 1991. *The Edwardian Theatre: Essays on Performance and the Stage*. Cambridge: Cambridge University Press.

Borthwick, Stuart, and Ron Moy. 2004. *Popular Music Genres: An Introduction*. Edinburgh: Edinburgh University Press.

Bracewell, Michael. 2008. *Re-make/re-model: Art, Pop, Fashion and the Making of Roxy Music, 1953–1972*. London: Faber and Faber.

Bruzzi, Stella, and Pamela Church Gibson. 2000. *Fashion Cultures: Theories, Explorations and Analysis*. London: Routledge.

Burns, Gary. 1996. "Popular music, television and generational identity." *Journal of Popular Culture* 30(3): 129–41.

Burton, Graeme. 2005. *Media and Society: Critical Perspectives*. Milton Keynes: Open University Press.

Butler, Judith. 1990. *Gender Trouble: Feminism and the Subversion of Identity.* New York: Routledge.

Carrigan, Marylyn, and Isabelle Szmigin. 2000. "Advertising in an ageing society." *Ageing and Society* 20(2): 217–233.

Chesky, Kris S. and Stephen Corns. 1999. *Income from Music Performance: Does Attending College make Cents?* Austin: TX: Texas Music Educators Association.

Cohen, Sara. 1991. *Rock Culture in Liverpool: Popular Music in the Making.* Oxford: Clarendon Press.

— 2005. "Screaming at The Moptops: convergences between tourism and popular music." In *The Media and the Tourist Imagination*, ed. David Crouch, Rona Jackson and Felix Thompson, pp. 76–91. London: Routledge.

Connell, John, and Chris Gibson. 2002. *Sound Tracks: Popular Music, Identity, and Place.* London: Routledge.

Connor Steven, ed. 2004. *The Cambridge Companion to Postmodernism.* Cambridge: Cambridge University Press.

Cook, Nicholas. 2003. "Music as Performance." In *The Cultural Study of Music: a Critical Introduction*, ed. M. Clayton, T. Herbert and R. Middleton, pp. 204–214. London: Routledge.

Cooper, Lee. 2005. "Tribute discs, career development, and death: perfecting the celebrity product from Elvis Presley to Stevie Ray." *Popular Music and Society*, 28(2): 229–248.

Cox, Jay. 1980. "The Last Day in the Life." *Time*, 22 December: 18–24.

Cox, Tom. 2007. "The Great Pretenders." *The Times*, 3 June.

Curtis, Jim. 1987. *Rock Eras: Interpretations of Music and Society,1954–1984.* Bowling Green, OH: Bowling Green State University Popular Press.

Danesi, Marcel. 2006. *Brands.* London: Routledge.

Darryl Chamberlain. 2000. "Tribute bands: The next best thing," http://news.bbc.co.uk/1/hi/in_depth/entertainment/2000/brit_awards/657042.stm, 29 February.

Denisoff, Serge. 1975. *Solid Gold: The Popular Record Industry.* New Brunswick, NJ: Transaction Publishers.

Doss, Erica. 1999. *Elvis Culture: Fans, Faith and Image.* Lawrence KS: University of Kansas Press.

Dunaway, David. 1987. "Music as Political Communication in United States." In James Lull, *Popular Music and Communication*, p. 36. London, Sage.

Durant, Alan. 1985. *Conditions of Music.* London: Macmillan.

Dutton, Denis, ed. 1983. *The Forger's Art: Forgery and the Philosophy of Art.* Berkeley, CA: University of California Press.

Dyer, Richard. 1979. *Stars*, London: British Film Institute.

Dyer, Richard. 1987. *Heavenly Bodies.* Macmillan: Basingstoke.

— 2004. *Heavenly Bodies: Film Stars and Society.* London: Routledge.

Eco, Umberto. 1986. *Faith in Fakes: Travels in Hyperreality.* Los Angeles, CA: University of California: Secker and Warburg.

Elliot, Anthony. 1999. *The Mourning of John Lennon.* Berkeley, CA: University of California Press.

Evans, Jessica, and David Hesmondhalgh, eds. 2005. *Understanding Media: Inside Celebrity.* Milton Keynes: Open University Press.

Everett, Walter. 2001. *The Beatles as Musicians: The Quarry Men through Rubber Soul.* New York: Oxford University Press.

Fairley, Jan, Simon Frith, Will Straw and John Street, eds. 2001. *The Cambridge Companion to Rock and Pop.* Cambridge: Cambridge University Press.

Ferrari, Giovanni, ed. 2000. *Plato: The Republic.* Cambridge: Cambridge University Press.

Finnegan, Ruth. 1989. *The Hidden Musicians: Music-Making in an English Town.* Cambridge: Cambridge University Press.

Fiske, John. 1989a. *Reading the Popular.* Boston, MA: Unwin and Hyman.

— 1989b. *Reading the Popular.* London: Routledge.

Fleming, Nic. 2007. "Rock and pop stars do 'live fast, die young'." *The Daily Telegraph*, 4 September.

Fornarow, Wendy. 2006. *Empire of Dirt: The Aesthetics and Rituals of British Indie Music.* Middletown, CT: Wesleyan University Press.

Frederickson, Jon, and James Rooney. 2005. "The Free-lance Musician as a Type of Non–Person: an Extension of the Concept of Non-Personhood." *Sociological Quarterly* 28(2): 221–239.

Friedman, Will. 2008. "Ghost Bands Very Much Alive." *The New York Times*, 7 February.

Frith, Simon. 1996 [1978]. "Youth Culture/Youth Cults: A Decade of Rock Consumption." In *And The Beat Goes On: The Rock File Reader*, ed. Charlie Gillett and Simon Frith, p. 150. London: Pluto.

— 1983. *Sound Effects: Youth, Leisure and the Politics of Rock 'n' Roll.* London: Constable.

— 1987a. "The Industrialisation of Popular Music." In *Popular Music and Communication*, ed. J. Lull, pp. 53–77. London: Sage.

— 1987b. "Why do songs have words?" In *Lost in Music: Culture, Style and the Musical Event*, ed. A. L. White, p. 97. London: Routledge.

— 1996a. "Introduction: Backward and Forward." In *The Beat Goes On: The Rock File Reader*, ed. Charlie Gillett and Simon Frith, pp. 1–8. London: Pluto.

— 1996b. *Performing Rites: On the Value of Popular Music.* Oxford: Oxford University Press.

Frith, Simon, and Lee Marshall. 2004. *Music and Copyright.* Edinburgh: Edinburgh University Press.

Frith, Simon, and Angela McRobbie. 1978. "Rock and Sexuality." *Screen Education* 19(9): 3–19.

Frith, Simon, and Andrew Goodwin. 1990. *On Record: Rock, Pop and the Written Word.* London: Routledge.

Frith, Simon, Will Straw and John Street, eds. 2001. *The Cambridge Companion to Pop and Rock.* Cambridge: Cambridge University Press.

Gabbard, Krin. 2004. *Black Magic: White Hollywood and African American Culture.* New Brunswick, NJ: Rutgers University Press.

Garofalo, Reebee. 1999. "From Music Publishing to MP3: Music and Industry in the Twentieth Century." *American Music* 15(3) (September): 318–354.

Goffman, Erving. 1956. *The Presentation of Self in Everyday Life.* New York: Doubleday.

— 1959. *The Presentation of Self in Everyday Life.* New York: Panetheon.

Goodwin, Andrew. 1988. "Sample and Hold: Pop Music in the Digital Age of Reproduction." *Critical Quarterly* 30(3): 37–38.

Gorman, Paul. 2001. *The Look: Adventures in Pop and Rock Fashion.* London: Sanctuary.

Gracyk, Theodore. 1996. *Rhythm and Noise: an Aesthetics of Rock*. Durham, NC: Duke University Press.

Gregson, Nicky, and Louise Crewe. 2003. *Second-Hand Cultures*. Oxford: Blackwell.

Greig, Charlotte. 1989. *Will You Still Love Me Tomorrow? Girl Groups from the 50s On*. London: Virago.

Grossberg, Lawrence. 1994. "Is anybody listening? Does anybody care? On the state of rock' in Hartley, John (1994) 'Genre' in Tim O'Sullivan (*et al.*), *Key Concepts in Communication and Cultural Studies*. London: Routledge.

Harkin, James, and Julia Huber. 2004. *Eternal Youths: How the Baby Boomers are Having their Time Again*. London: Demos.

Haslam, Dave. 2000. "What the Twist Did for the Peppermint Lounge." *London Review of Books*, http://www.lrb.co.uk/v22/n01/hasl02_.html.

Haughey, Nuala. 1996. "Fans are back in town to recall Lynott." *The Irish Times*, 5 January.

Hebdige, Dick. 1979. *Subculture: the Meaning of Style*. London: Routledge.

Hermes, Jouke. 1995. *Reading Women's Magazines: an Analysis of Everyday Media Use*. London: Polity.

Hesmondhalgh, David. 2002. "Popular music audiences and everyday life." In David Hesmondhalgh and Matt Hills eds. *Fan Cultures*. London: Routledge.

Hickey, Dave. 1997. *Air Guitar: Essays on Art and Democracy*. Los Angeles, CA: Art Issues Press.

Hitchcock, Robyn. 2006. "He Can't Sing." *Word* (January): 89, www.wordmagazine.co.uk.

Holmes, Thom. 2002. *Electronic and Experimental Music* (2nd edn). New York: Routledge.

Holt, Fabian. 2007. *Genre in Popular Music*. Chicago, IL: University of Chicago Press.

Homan, Shane, ed. 2006. *Access All Eras: Tribute Bands and Global Pop Culture*. Maidenhead: Open University Press.

Horner, Bruce, and Thomas Swiss. 2000. *Key Terms in Popular Music and Culture*. Oxford: Blackwell.

Hull, Geoffrey. 2004. *The Recording Industry*. London: Routledge.

Huyssen, Andreas. 1986. *After the Great Divide: Modernism, Mass Culture, Postmodernism*. Bloomington, IN: Indiana University Press.

Isnard, Guy. 1960) *Faux et Imitations Dans L'Art* (vol. 2). Paris: Arthème Fayard.

Jameson, Frederick. 1983. "Postmodernism and Consumer Society." In Hal Foster ed. *Postmodern Culture*, p. 115. London: Pluto.

— 1988. "Postmodernism and Consumer Society." In Ann Gray and Jim McGuigan eds. *Studies in Culture: An Introductory Reader*. London: Arnold.

Jenkins, Henry. 1992. *Textual Poachers: Television Fans and Participatory Culture*. New York: Routledge.

Jones, Mablen. 1987. *Getting it On: the Clothing of Rock and Roll*. New York: Abbeville.

Jones, Mark, ed. 1990). *Fake? The Art of Deception*. Berkeley, CA: University of California Press.

Jourard, Marty. 1998. "Tribute Bands: Close Enough for Rock 'n' Roll". *Gig Magazine*, November.

Kaplan, E. Ann. 1987. *Rockin' Around the Clock: Music, Television and Consumer Culture*. London: Methuen.

Kearney, Mary Celeste. 1985. "Teenagers and Television in the United States." In Horace Newcomb ed. *Museum of Broadcast Communications Encyclopedia of Television*, pp. 2276–281. New York: Fitzroy Dearborn.

Knabb, Ken, ed. 1981. *Situationist International Anthology*. Berkeley, CA: Bureau of Public Secrets.

Krasner, David. 2000. *Method Acting Reconsidered: Theory, Practice, Future*. Basingstoke: Palgrave Macmillan.

Kubler-Ross, Elisabeth. 1973. *On Death and Dying*. London: Routledge.

Kurutz, Steven. 2008. *Like A Rolling Stone: The Strange Life of A Tribute Band*. New York: Random House.

Kurz, Otto. 1979. *Art Forgeries and How to Examine Paintings Scientifically*. Albuquerque, NM: Gloucester Art Press.

Kusek, David, and Gerd Leonhard. 2005. *The Future of Music: Manifesto for the Digital Music Revolution*. Boston, MA: Berklee.

Kusek, David, and Leonhard Gerd. 2005. *The Future of Music: Manifesto for the Digital Music Revolution*. Boston, MA: Berklee Press.

Lacan, Jacques. 1977 [1966]. *Ecrits: A Selection*, trans. Alan Sheridan. New York: Norton.

Lawson, Colin, and Robin Stowell. 1999. *The Historical Performance of Music: An Introduction*. Cambridge: Cambridge University Press.

Leadbeater, Charles, and Kate Oakley. 1999. *The Independents: Britain's New Cultural Entrepreneurs*, London: Demos.

Levy, Joe. 2003. *Rolling Stone's 500 Greatest Albums of All Time*. New York: Wenner Books.

Lewis, David. 1991. *Led Zeppelin: a Celebration*. London: Omnibus.

Livingston, Tamara, E. 1997. "Musical Revivals: Towards a General Theory." *Ethnomusicology* 43(1) (Winter): 66–85.

Lowenthal, David *The Past is a Foreign Country*. Cambridge: Cambridge University Press

Malone, Matthew.2008 [2003/2004]. "Facing the Music." *Conde Nast Portfolio Magazine*, March.

Martin, Peter. 1995. *Sounds and Society: Themes in the Sociology of Music*. Manchester: Manchester University Press.

Mayer Brown, Howard. 1988. "Pedantary or Liberation? A Sketch of the Historical Performance Movement." In N. Kenyon ed. *Authenticity and Early Music: a Symposium*. Oxford: Oxford University Press.

McLaughlin, Noel. 2001. "Rock, Fashion and Performativity." In Stella Bruzzi and Pamela Church-Gibson eds. *Fashion Cultures: Theories, Explorations and Analysis*. London: Routledge.

Meyer, Moe, ed. 1994. *The Politics and Poetics of Camp*. London: Routledge.

Middleton, Richard. 1990. *Studying Popular Music*. Milton Keynes: Open University Press.

Mirzoeff, Nicholas. 1998. "What is Visual Culture." In *The Visual Culture Reader*. New York: Routledge.

MORI. 2004. A survey of live music staged in England and Wales. Department of Culture, Media and Sport (September).

Morrow, Guy. 2006. "Selling out or buying in? The dual career of the original and cover band musician." In S. Homan ed. *Access All Eras: Tribute Bands and Global Pop Culture*. Maidenhead: Open University Press.

Muendel, Jef. 2008. "The Australian Pink Floyd: A Band from Down Under Imitate Roger Waters and Company." Suite 101.com, 15 September, classicrockmusic70s90s.suite101.com.

Mundy, Julie. 2003. *Elvis Fashion: from Memphis to Vegas*. New York: Universe Publishing.

Negus, Keith. 1999. *Music Genres and Corporate Culture*. London: Routledge.

Negus, Keith. 2001. *Producing Pop: Culture and Conflict in the Popular Music Industry*. London: Arnold.

Negus, Keith, eds. 2002. *Popular Music Studies*. London: Arnold.

Noble, Douglas. 2004. "Australian Pink Floyd Workshop." *Guitar & Bass Magazine* (January).

Nowotny, Helga. 2003. "Democratising expertise and socially robust knowledge." *Science and Public Policy* 30: 151–156.

Owram, Doug. 1997. *Born at the Right Time: A History of the Baby Boom Generation*. Toronto: University of Toronto Press.

Parker, Nick. 1996. "On Tribute Bands." *The Independent*, 27 October 2006.

Patel, Raj. 2001. "Booking Your UK Tribute Band." *Tribute City*, www.tributecity.com/archives.php?action=article&id=4

Peterson, Richard A. and David G. Berger. 1975. "Cycles in symbol production: the case of popular music." *American Sociological Review* 40: 158–173.

Petridis, Alex. 2007. "The copycats who got the cream." *The Guardian*, 18 May.

Phillips, Sarah. 2007. "Did a lack of teenagers ruin this year's Glastonbury?" *The Guardian*, 13 July.

Plasketes, George. 2005. "Re-flections on the Cover Age: A Collage of Continuous Coverage." *Popular Music and Society* 2: 137–161.

Plato. 2004. *Ion*, Whitefish, MT: Kessinger Publishing.

Popa, Christopher. 2004. "Do Big Bands Today Stand a 'Ghost' of a Chance?" www.bigbandlibrary.com.

Popoff, Martin. 1997. *The Collectors Guide to Heavy Metal*. Burlington: Collectors Guide Publishing.

Rank, Otto. 1971. *The Double: A Psychoanalytical Study*. Chapel Hill, NC: University of North Carolina Press.

Redhead, Steve. 1990. *The End-of-the-Century Party: Youth and Pop towards 2000*. Manchester: Manchester University Press.

Reinholtz, R. 1991. "Sex and gender issues in American pop music." Paper presented at the National meeting of the Society for the Scientific Study of Sex in New Orleans, Louisiana.

Rentfrow, P. J. and Gosling, S. D. 2007. "The content and validity of music-genre stereotypes among college students." *Psychology of Music*, 35, 306–326.

Rice, Jo, and David Roberts, eds. 2000, *Guinness Book of British Hit Singles* (13th Edition), London: Guinness World Records Ltd.

Richter, Linda. 2004. "The Politics of Heritage Tourism Development." In *Heritage, Museums and Galleries: an Introductory Reader*, ed. Gerard Corsane, pp. 282–298. London: Routledge.

Ricoeur, Paul. 2004. *Memory, History, Forgetting*. Chicago, IL: Chicago University Press.

Riley, Mykaell, and Dave Laing. 2006. *The Value of Jazz in Britain*. London: University of Westminster.

Robertson, Pamela. 1996. *Guilty Pleasures: Feminist Camp from Mae West to Madonna*. London: I. B. Taurus.

Rodman, Gilbert. 1996. *Elvis after Elvis: the Posthumous Career of a Living Legend*. London: Routledge.

Rogers, Robert. 1970. *A Psychoanalytic Study of the Double in Literature*. Detroit, MI: Wayne State University Press.

Rosenbaum, Ron. 1995. "Among the Believers." *The New York Times*, 24 September.

Ross, Andrew, and Tricia Rose, eds. 1994. *Microphone Fiends: Youth Music and Youth Culture*, pp. 54–55. London: Routledge.

Ruhlmann, William. 2004. *Breaking Records: 100 Years of Hits*. London: Routledge.

Sandvoss, Cornel. 2005. *Fans*. Cambridge: Polity Press.

Sanjek, Russell, and David Sanjek. 1991. *American Popular Music Business in the Twentieth Century*. New York: Oxford University Press.

Santoro, Gene. 1995. *Dancing in Your Head: Jazz, Blues, Rock, and Beyond*. Oxford: Oxford University Press.

Savage, George. 1963. *Forgeries, Fakes, and Reproductions, a Handbook For the Collector*. London: Barrie and Rockliff.

Savage, Jon. 1990 [1988]. "The enemy within: sex, rock and identity." In Simon Frith ed. *Facing the Music: Essays on Pop, Rock and Culture*, 2nd edn. London: Mandarin.

Schechner, Richard. 2006. *Performance Studies: An Introduction*. London: Routledge.

Schwartz, Hillel. 1996. *The Culture of the Copy: Striking Likenesses, Unreasonable Facsimiles*. New York: Zone.

Sedgwick, Eve. 1985. *Between Men: English Literature and Male Homosocial Desire*. New York: Columbia University Press.

Sheppard, Anne. 1987. *Aesthetics: An Introduction to the Philosophy of Art*. Oxford: Oxford University Press.

Sherwood, James. 2003. "Who are the real fashion victims?" The *Independent*, 13 October.

Shipton, Alyn. 2009. *I Feel a Song Coming On*. Chicago, IL: University of Illinois Press.

Shuker, Roy. 1994. *Understanding Popular Music*. London: Routledge.

— 2002. *Understanding Popular Music*. London: Routledge.

— 2008. *Understanding Popular Music Culture*. London: Routledge.

Sims, Josh. 1999. *Rock Fashion*. London: Omnibus.

Spiegel, Lynn. 1990. "Communicating with the dead. Elvis as Medium." *Camera Obscura* 23: 176–205.

Stark, Phyllis. 1994. "A History of Radio Broadcasting." *Billboard*, 1 November, p. 4.

Storey, John. 2001. *Cultural Theory and Popular Culture: an Introduction*. London: Prentice Hall.

Strausbaugh, John. 2001. *Rock Till You Drop*. London: Verso.

Straw, Will. 1993. "Popular Music and Postmodernism in the 1980s." In L. Grossberg and A. Goodwin eds. *Sound and Vision: The Music Video Reader*. London: Routledge.

— 1997. "Sizing Up Record Collections: Gender and Connoisseurship in Rock Music Culture." In Sheila Whiteley ed. *Sexing the Groove: Popular Music and Gender*. pp. 3–16. London: Routledge.

— 1999. "Authorship." In B. Horner, and T. Swiss eds. *Key Terms in Popular Music and Culture*. Oxford: Blackwell.

— 2000. "Exhausted Commodities: The Material Culture of Music." *Canadian Journal of Communication* 25(1): 175–185.

Street Porter, Janet. 2002. "Jubilee!" *The Independent*, 26 May.

Strickland, Lucy. 1995. "The Boys are Really Back in Town." *Loaded* (October): 15.

Tarlach, Gemma. 2002. "Highway to History: Tribute Bands Rock out Salutes to the Likes of AC/DC, KISS." *Milwaukee Journal Sentinel*, 29 August.

Taruskin, Richard. 1995. *Text and Act: Essays on Music and Performance*. Oxford: Oxford University Press.

Theberge, Paul. 1997. *Any Sound You Can Imagine: Making Music/Consuming Technology*. Hanover, NH: Wesleyan University Press and the University Press of New England.

Thornton, Sarah. 1990. "Strategies for reconstructing the popular past." *Popular Music* 9.1 (January): 87–95.

Trynka, Paul, ed. 2004. *The Beatles: 10 Years That Shook the World*. London: Dorling Kindersley.

Tucker, Mark. 1999. "Mainstreaming Monk: The Ellington Album." *Black Music Research Journal* 19.2: 227–33. Chicago, IL: Columbia College.

Turino, Thomas. 2008. *Music as Social Life: the Politics of Participation*. Chicago, IL: Chicago University Press.

Turow, Joseph. 2008. *Niche Envy: Marketing Discrimination in the Digital Age*. Cambridge: MIT Press.

Vasari, Georgio. 1998. *The Lives of the Artists*. Oxford: Oxford University Press.

Vermorel, Fred, and Judy Vermorel. 1985. *Starlust: The Secret Fantasies of Fans*. London: Comet.

Waldrep, Shelton. 2004. *The Aesthetics of Self-Invention: Oscar Wilde to David Bowie*. Minneapolis, MN: University of Minnesota Press.

Wall, Tim. 2003. *Studying Popular Music Culture*. London: Arnold.

Walser, Robert. 1993. *Running With the Devil: Power, Gender and Madness in Heavy Metal Music*. Hanover, NH: Wesleyan University Press.

Weinstein, Deena. 1991. *Heavy Metal: A Cultural Sociology*. New York: Lexington.

— 2000. *Heavy Metal: the Music and Its Culture*. New York: da Capo.

Wells, Alan. 1990. "Popular Music: Emotional Use and Management." *Journal of Popular Culture* 24(1): 105–117.

Williams, Dick. 1957. "6000 Kids Cheer Elvis' Frantic Sex Show." *The Daily Mirror*, 29 October.

Williams, M. 1988. "Floyd Droids." *Lighting Dimensions*, January/February (www.via-internet.com/).

Willis, Paul. 1978. *Profane Culture*. London: Routledge.

— 1990. *Common Culture: Symbolic Work at Play in the Everyday Cultures of the Young*. Milton Keynes: Open University Press.

Wills, Geoff, and Cary L. Cooper. 1988. *Pressure Sensitive: Popular Musicians Under Stress*. London: Sage.

Wincentsen, Ed. 2002. *Yes, Phoenix had Music in the Sixties! A Look at the Clubs, Bands and the Fans*. Pickens: Momentary Pleasures Press.

Woods, Gregory, and Tim Franks. 2006. "Music, Film and Post-Stonewall Gay Identity." In Ian Conrich and Estelle Tincknell eds. *Films Musical Moments*, pp. 158–169. Edinburgh: Edinburgh University Press.

Woods, Tim. 1999. *Beginning Postmodernism*. Manchester: Manchester University Press.

Zuben, Nabeel. 2001. *Sounds English: Transnational Popular Music*. Chicago, IL: University of Illinois Press.

Index